THREE GREEK PLAYS

Books by EDITH HAMILTON

THE ROMAN WAY

THE GREEK WAY

THE PROPHETS OF ISRAEL

THREE GREEK PLAYS

THREE GREEK PLAYS

PROMETHEUS BOUND
AGAMEMNON
THE TROJAN WOMEN

TRANSLATED WITH INTRODUCTIONS BY

EDITH HAMILTON

W · W · NORTON & COMPANY · INC.
PUBLISHERS · NEW YORK

CONTENTS

v

THREE GREEK PLAYS

I

ON TRANSLATING

wwwwwwwwwwwwwwwwwwwwwwwwwwwwwwwwwwwwwwwwwwww

WHAT IS A TRANS-
lation? What ought a translator to aim at? The two
most distinguished translators of comparatively modern times are Browning and FitzGerald of Omar
Khayyám fame, both of whom translated the *Agamemnon* of Aeschylus. In FitzGerald's version, Clytemnestra's first speech, four lines in the original, all
spoken by Clytemnestra, appears thus:

CLYTEMNESTRA

Oh never yet did Night—
Night of all Good the Mother, as men say,
Conceive a fairer issue than To-day!
Prepare your ear, Old Man, for tidings such
As youthful hope would scarce anticipate.

CHORUS

I have prepared them for such news as such
Preamble argues.

CLYTEMNESTRA

What if you be told—
Oh, mighty sum in one small figure cast!—
That ten-year-toiled-for Troy is ours at last?

Browning turns it into:

Good-news-announcer, may—as is the byword—
Morn become, truly—news from Night his mother!
But thou shalt learn joy past all hope of hearing.
Priamos' city‚have the Argeioi taken.

And the only share Aeschylus has in these two per-
formances is,

With glad tidings, so the proverb runs,
May dawn arise from the kind mother, night.
For you shall learn a joy beyond all hope.
The Greeks have taken Priam's city.

This is undoubtedly discouraging to people unable to read Greek but interested in getting some
idea of what the poetry is like which has still never
been surpassed. One would certainly suppose that
the ideal translator of a Greek tragedy would be a
great poet and a Greek scholar combined, who could
keep a masterpiece a masterpiece while putting it au-
thentically into another language. But Browning's
Agamemnon is beyond question one of the worst
translations ever made, and FitzGerald's, whose
Omar has been called much too good to be a good
translation, is equally deficient as a translation, but
by no means because it is too good.

So far the poets have not helped. Their endow-
ment seems rather to lead them along their own lines
and away from their original. Even Professor Gil-

bert Murray, who resurrected Greek tragedy lying dead on the scholars' bookshelves, but—are we to say?—has undoubtedly a poetic gift, will turn that simple and unadorned speech of Clytemnestra's into,

> Glad-voiced, the old saw telleth, comes this morn,
> The Star-child of a dancing midnight born.
> And beareth to thine ear a word of joy
> Beyond all hope: the Greek hath taken Troy.

There is clearly something to be said for translators who are not poets. Their only possible reason for translating is that they care enough for the original to make an attempt to put it into English—which implies, really, quite a devoted love—and, since they are aware of their own poetic deficiencies, they will try to follow humbly the actual words of what they feel is so great. But, of course, such people will never be able to reproduce the glory of the Greek. The best they write will be only a dim reflection.

What are they to try for? Not a complete literal fidelity. Du Maurier has shown the dangers of that ideal.

Cassez-vous, cassez-vous, cassez-vous, sur vos froids gris cailloux, O mer.

And Pope's literal rendering of three lines in Homer is, so far as my knowledge goes, quite unsurpassed in the long records of atrocious translations,

> Tears his cheeks bedewed.
> Nor less the father poured a social flood.
> They wept abundant and they wept aloud.

No: a bald word-for-word translation of a Greek play would accomplish nothing at all. The reader would not get the least idea of what the play was like.

"As faithful as it can, as free as it must," is a German critic's contribution. Ah, but the point is, in what does faithfulness consist? Is one to be faithful first to the text, or to that indefinable something we call the spirit? It has been said that Aeschylus "does somehow spoil one's taste for twitterings." Undoubtedly a translator, however accurate verbally, would be guilty of the great betrayal if he made him twitter. On the other hand, as Professor Postgate says, himself a distinguished translator, "Fidelity to the spirit is often invoked to excuse infidelity to the text."

Also, there is this to be said: fidelity to the text is quite possible, but can one be sure of being faithful to the spirit? The heights on which the spirits of the supreme poets dwell, whether they wrote in English or Greek, are inaccessible to most of us. I believe that the best a translator can hope for on that point is to convey some of his own enthusiasm, something of the impression the poem made upon him, which certainly will never be profound enough to contain adequately all that the poem means. His enthusiasm, however, will be regulated by a careful regard for the way his original writes, if he has no confidence in his own poetic power to say it better.

Fidelity to the text is, however, by no means an easy matter to judge. If only we could return to those days of verbal unanimity when, the ancient record says, the seventy translators of the Old Testament into Greek, "shut up in seventy separate cells produced independently translations identical in every word from first to last." But never since that paradise of translators has there been any agreement at all between any two people who translate.

The literal translation of the first verse of the first choral song in *The Trojan Women* runs: "About Ilium sing to me, O Muse, with tears, an ode for the grave, of strange songs, for now I will loudly utter melody for Troy."

To my mind I am translating this faithfully when I write,

> Sing me, O Muse, a song for Troy,
> a strange song sung to tears,
> a music for the grave.
> O lips, sound forth a melody
> for Troy.

It is true that Aeschylus does not use *lips*, but the word he does use, meaning to cry out or speak loudly, is made up of three heavy syllables to which "lips sound forth" is a fair equivalent. I think my lines are quite accurate.

But of course Professor Murray thinks the same of his when he writes,

> O Muse, be near me now, and make
> A strange song for Ilium's sake,
> Till a tone of tears be about my ears
> And out of my lips a music break
> For Troy, Troy, and the end of the years.

And, presumably, the Loeb Classical Library people have the same opinion about their translator:

> O Song-goddess, chant in mine ear
>   The doom of mine Ilium: sing

Thy strange notes broken with sob and tear
That o'er sepulchres sigh where our dear dead lie:
For now through my lips outwailing clear
  Troy's ruin-dirge shall ring—

We are far indeed from that happy time when the Seventy all upheld each other and no reader had to be puzzled to make a choice.

For myself, in my own translations I want to be accurate more than I want to be readable—although I recognize fully that if I make Aeschylus and Euripides dull or ugly, I have done the most unpardonable thing a translator can do. Nevertheless I should not dare to add a thought of my own to these mighty masters in order to make it easier for the reader to understand them or to discover the beauty and the grandeur of what I can put so inadequately before him. If Euripides does not speak of sighing over sepulchres where the dear dead lie, then I will not.

Professor Murray has said that the Greek mode of expression would often seem so bald as to antagonize a reader if it were rendered literally, and that he prefers, then, to give a richer, more decorated expression, in accordance with the genius of English poetry; but I believe that his idea dates from the Victorian poets, and that today when Tennyson and Swinburne have lost their spell, English poetry is drawing closer to the simplicity and directness of the Greek. A modern translator's task is easier. The odds are that his reader will not be put off by plain writing.

It is the special hardship of a translator's lot that he, far more than all other writers, is unable to be a judge of his work, to know whether he is, in some measure, the interpreter of the beauty he is so keenly aware of, or misrepresenting and distorting it.

Years ago Professor Murray wrote words so arresting and so true that they make a perfect apologia for any translation and might well be the preface to every one: "A translator cannot help seeing his own work through the medium of the greater thing which he studies and loves. The light of the original shines through it and the music of the original echoes round it. Creech's versions of Horace and Theocritus may possess as little 'art of speech' as their famous critic implies, the Horace no Horace of ours and the Theocritus utterly unlike Theocritus. But to Creech himself how different it all was! He did not feel any veil of intervening Creech. To him the Theocritus was something haunted by all the magic of Theocritus. When he read his baldest lines his voice, no doubt, trembled with emotion. But it was the original that caused the emotion. The original was always there present to him in a kind of symbol; its beauty, perhaps, even increased by that idealization and endearment which naturally attend the long and loving service of one human mind to another."

So far, there has never been a really great translation of a Greek play, none which, like the English Bible, sweeps away all consciousness of any original other than the English words, so beautiful and so moving that the mind refuses to go back of them. Greek translations become quickly dated.

Until the perfect, the final, translator comes, the plays should be perpetually retranslated for each generation. The present volume presents three of the greatest Greek tragedies translated into approximately the modern idiom. The two plays of Aeschylus, *Prometheus* and *Agamemnon*, show best the range of his genius. The third play, *The Trojan Women* of Euripides, is the most modern in feeling of all Greek tragedies.

There are few efforts more conducive to humility than that of the translator trying to communicate an incommunicable beauty. Yet, unless we do try, something unique and never surpassed will cease to exist except in the libraries of a few inquisitive book-lovers.

In this present enterprise, to give to three of the greatest of poetic dramas a temporary English life, the translator begs the help of the reader in re-creating a past when tragedy was a purifying rite as well as a source of interest and emotion; a searching into the mystery of the universe as well as into the puzzle of the human heart. The obstacle of a different world added to that of a different language cannot be surmounted by the writer alone. "Piece out our imperfections with your thoughts."

II

METERS

⎍⎍⎍

In THE TRANSLA-
tions of *The Trojan Women* and *Prometheus* I have
not tried to keep the original meters anywhere, as
I have done in the choruses of *Agamemnon*. In the
dialogue of a Greek play the meter used was always
a line with six accents. In English poetry this line is
rarely found, and for the most part at the end of a
verse, where it has the effect of a pause in the poem.

> And in the midst, 'mong thousand heraldries,
> And twilight saints, and dim emblazonings,
> A shielded scutcheon blushed with blood of
>   queens and kings.

The last line is the exact numerical equivalent of the
line used in the Greek dialogue, but it is not the aes-
thetic equivalent. The English is slow and weighty;
the Greek is light and swift. A line with five accents,
like the first two lines of the quotation, is far nearer
to the effect of the Greek, and in general it has been

adopted by translators. I have followed them, but only to a limited extent. I have not held myself bound to any fixed meter. Nor have I made any attempt to keep all the lines the same length. In a Greek play the dialogue runs on unbroken, with hardly ever a line cut short. But in a translation the use of a line of varying length sets the translator free from the necessity of padding. Words and even whole sentences have often to be added if each line must invariably be as long as the others—as witness all the translators who have felt that necessity. In such translations a reader, ignorant of Greek, can never feel any certainty whether a word or a phrase or a sentence is the poet's or only a makeshift required to fill out the line. This serious disadvantage is never counterbalanced by reproducing the Greek meter. No translator, as far as I know, has done this.

The meter of a Greek chorus, however, is always irregular, and often to an astonishing degree. In one of the choruses of the *Prometheus* a seven-syllable line is followed by a line of twenty-four syllables. The accent, too, may vary from line to line. In using an irregular line scheme a translator cannot be accused of doing something that is alien to the genius of Greek poetry.

It is hardly necessary to add that rhyme was not used by the Greek tragedians. To rhyme Aeschylus is like rhyming Isaiah.

III

A PACIFIST
IN PERICLEAN ATHENS

THE GREATEST
piece of anti-war literature there is in the world was
written 2,350 years ago. This is a statement worth
a thought or two. Nothing since, no description or
denunciation of war's terrors and futilities, ranks
with *The Trojan Women*, which was put upon the
Athenian stage by Euripides in the year 416 B. C. In
that faraway age a man saw with perfect clarity
what war was, and wrote what he saw in a play of
surpassing power, and then—nothing happened. No
one was won over to his side—no band of eager dis-
ciples took up his idea and went preaching it to a
war-ridden world. That superlatively efficient war-
machine, Rome, described by one of her own his-
torians as having fought continuously for eight hundred years, went on to greater and greater efficiency,
with never a glimmer from Euripides to disturb her

complacency. In the long annals of literature no
writer is recorded who took over his point of view.
A few objectors to war are known to us. They crop
out sporadically through the ages, but rarely and
never with Euripides' deliberate intention of show-
ing war up for what it is. And except for Christ, to
whom non-resistance was fundamental, we do not
know of anyone else who disbelieved in violence as
a means of doing good. None of Christ's followers
seem to have followed Him there until comparatively modern times. Not one medieval saint stands
out to oppose the thousands of saintly believers in
the holiness of this war or that. One soldier there was
in the early days of Christianity, a simple, uneducated
man, who refused to fight when he was converted,
because, as he explained, Christ did not approve of
men killing each other. But he was easily silenced—
and the Church never denounced his executioners.
He never came near to being made a saint. His very
name, Marcellus, is known only to the curious. That
was doctrine too dangerous for the Fathers of the
Church. Christians refuse to fight? Rather, set up a
cross as the banner of a triumphant army, conquering under that standard, killing in His name.

The men of religion, along with the men of letters, passed by, unseeing, the road Euripides had
opened, and each usually vied with the other in glori-
fying and magnifying noble, heroic and holy war.

Consider the greatest of all, Shakespeare. He never
bothered to think war through. Of course, that was
not his way with anything. He had another method.
Did he believe in "Contumelious, beastly, mad-

brain'd war"? Or in "Pride, pomp and circumstance of glorious war"? He says as much on the one side as on the other.

"We few, we happy few, we band of brothers," King Henry cries before Agincourt:

> This day is called the feast of Crispian;
> And gentlemen of England now abed
> Shall think themselves accursed they were not here,
> And hold their manhoods cheap whiles any speaks
> That fought with us upon Saint Crispin's day.

And then a few pages on:

> If impious war
> Array'd in flames like to the Prince of fiends,
> Do, with his smirched complexion, all fell feats
> Enlink'd to waste and desolation—

It is not possible to know what Shakespeare really thought about war, if he really thought about it at all. Always that disconcerting power of imagination blocks the way to our knowledge of him. He saw eye to eye with Henry on one page and with the citizens of Harfleur on the next, and what he saw when he looked only for himself, he did not care to record.

In our Western world Euripides stands alone. He understood what the world has only begun today to understand.

"The burden of the valley of vision," wrote Isaiah, when he alone knew what could save his world from ruin. To perceive an overwhelmingly important truth of which no one else sees a glimmer, is loneliness such as few even in the long history of the world can have had to suffer. But Euripides suffered it for the greater part of his long life. The valley of vision was his abiding place.

He was the youngest of the three Greek tragic poets, but only a few years younger than Sophocles, who, indeed, survived him. The difference between the two men was great. Each had the keen discernment and the profound spiritual perception of the supreme artist. Each lived and suffered through the long-drawn-out war, which ended in the crushing defeat of Athens, and together they watched the human deterioration brought about during those years. But what they saw was not the same. Sophocles never dreamed of a world in which such things could not be. To him the way to be enabled to endure what was happening, the only way for a man to put life through no matter what happened, was to face facts unwaveringly and accept them, to perceive clearly and bear steadfastly the burden of the human lot, which is as it is and never will be different. To look at the world thus, with profundity, but in tranquillity of spirit, without bitterness, has been given to few, and to no other writer so completely as to Sophocles.

But Euripides saw clearest of all not what is, but what might be. So rebels are made. Great rebels all know the valley of vision. They see possibilities: this evil and that ended; human life transformed; people good and happy. "And there shall be neither sorrow nor crying, nor any more pain: for the former things are passed away." The clarity with which they see brings them anguish; they have a passion of longing to make their vision a reality. They feel, like a personal experience, the giant agony of the world. Not many among the greatest stand higher than Euripides in this aristocracy of humanity.

Sophocles said, "Nothing is wrong which gods command." Euripides said, "If gods do evil, then they are not gods." Two different worlds are outlined in those two ideas. Submission is the rule of the first. Not ours to pass judgment upon the divine. "There are thoughts too great for mortal men," was ever Sophocles' idea, or, in the words of another great Greek writer, "To long for the impossible is a disease of the soul." Keep then within the rational limit; "Sail not beyond the pillars of Heracles." But in the second world, Euripides' world, there can be no submission, because what reigns there is a passion for justice and a passion of pity for suffering. People who feel in that way do not submit to the inevitable, or even really perceive it. But they perceive intolerably what is wrong and under that tremendous impetus they are ready to throw all security aside, to call everything into question, to tear off the veils that hide ugly things, and often, certainly in Euripides' case, to give up forever peace of mind.

Two years before the end of the war Euripides died, not in Athens, but away up north in savage Thrace, lonelier in his death even than in his life. The reason he left his city is not recorded, but it was a compelling one. Men did not give up their home in Greek and Roman days unless they must. All we are told is a single sentence in the ancient *Life of Euripides* that he had to go away because of "the malicious exultation" aroused against him in the city. It is not hard to discover why.

Athens was fighting a life-and-death war. She did not want to think about anything. Soldiers must not think. If they begin to reason why, it is very bad for the army. Above all, they must not think about the rights and wrongs of the war. Athens called that being unpatriotic, not to say traitorous, just as emphatically as the most Aryan Nazi today could. And Euripides kept making her think. He put play after play on the stage which showed the hideousness of cruelty and the pitifulness of human weakness and human pain. The Athenians took their theater very seriously, and they were as keen and as sensitive an audience as has ever been in the world. It was unheard of in Athens to forbid a play because it was not in accordance with the ruling policy, but many a politician must have felt very uneasy as he listened to what Euripides had to say.

The war lasted twenty-seven years. Thucydides, the great historian of the time, remarks that "War, teaching men by violence, fits their characters to their condition," and two of his austere black-laid-on-white pictures illustrate with startling clarity how quickly the Athenians went downhill under that teaching.

They had been fighting for three years only when an important island in the Aegean revolted. Athens sent a big fleet against her and captured her, and in furious anger voted to put all the men to death and make slaves of the women and children. They dispatched a ship to carry the order to the general in command, and then, true to the spirit of the city that was still so great, they realized the shocking thing they had done, and they sent another boat to try to overtake the first and bring it back, or, if that was impossible, to get to the island in time to prevent the massacre. We are told how the rowers rowed as none ever before, and how they did arrive in time. And Athens felt that weight of guilt lifted, and rejoiced.

But as the war went on men did not feel guilty when terrible deeds were done. They grew used to them. Twelve years later, when the war had lasted fifteen years, another island offended Athens, not by revolting, only by trying to keep neutral. It was a tiny island, in itself of no importance, but by that time Athens was incapable of weighing pros and cons. She took the island, she killed all the men and enslaved all the women and children, and we hear of no one who protested. But a few months later one man showed what he thought, not only of this terrible deed but of the whole horrible business of war. Euripides brought out *The Trojan Women*.

There is no plot in *The Trojan Women* and almost no action. After a ten-year war a town has been taken by storm and the men in it killed. Except for two subordinate parts the characters are all women. Their husbands are dead, their children taken from them, and they are waiting to be shipped off to slavery. They talk about what has happened and how they feel, and this talk makes up the substance of the play. They are very unlike each other, so that we see the situation from different points of view. There is the wife of the king, an old woman, whose husband was cut down before her eyes, in their home as he clung to the altar; her sons, too, are dead, and she, a queen, is to be a slave to the conquerors. There is her daughter, a holy virgin, dedicated to the service of the god of truth, now to be the concubine of the victorious commander-in-chief. Her daughter-in-law too, wife of her dearest and most heroic son, she is to belong to the son of the man who killed him and misused him after death. Helen, the beautiful, is there as well, maneuvering to regain her power over the husband she betrayed, but, in the play, unsuccessful and led away to die. And there are a number of other women, not great or impressive at all except through their sufferings, pitiful creatures weeping for the loss of home, husband, children, and everything sweet and pleasant gone forever.

That is the whole of it. Not one gleam of light anywhere. Euripides had asked himself what war is like when one looks straight at it, and this is his answer. He knew his Homer. It was the Greek Bible. And that theme of glorious poetry about the dauntless deeds of valiant men, heroically fighting for the most beautiful woman in the world, turns in his hands into a little group of broken-hearted women.

A soldier from the victorious army, who comes to bring them orders, is surprised and irritated to find himself moved to pity them; but he shrugs his shoulders and says, "Well—that's war."

The pomp and pride and glorious circumstance are all gone. When the play opens it is just before dawn, and the only light in the darkness comes fitfully from the burning city. Against that background two gods talk to each other and at once Euripides makes clear what he thinks about war as a method of improving life in any way for anyone.

In the old stories about what happened after Troy fell, told for hundreds of years before Euripides, curiously the conquering Greeks did not come off well. They had an exceedingly bad voyage back, and even those who escaped storm and shipwreck found terrible things waiting for them at home. In those faraway times, long before history began, it would seem that some men had learned what our world hardly yet perceives, that inevitably victors and vanquished must in the end suffer together. It was one of those strange prophetic insights which occasionally disturb the sluggish flow of the human spirit, but seem to accomplish nothing for centuries of time. Euripides, however, had discovered the meaning behind the stories.

He makes his two gods decide that the fall of Troy shall turn out no better for the Greeks than for the Trojans. "Give the Greek ships a bitter homecoming," Athena, once the ally of the Greeks, says fiercely to the god of the sea. He agrees that when they set sail for Greece he will "make the wild Aegean roar until shores and reefs and cliffs will hold dead men, bodies of many dead," and when she leaves him he meditates for a moment on human folly: "The fools, who lay a city waste, so soon to die themselves."

"Mother," the Trojan queen's daughter says, "I will show you,

"This town, now, yes, Mother,
is happier than the Greeks—
They came here to the banks of the Scamander,
and tens of thousands died. For what?
No man had moved their land-marks
or laid siege to their high-walled towns.
But those whom war took never saw their children.
No wife with gentle hand shrouded them for their
    grave.
They lie in a strange land. And in their homes
are sorrows too, the very same.
Lonely women who died. Old men who waited
for sons that never came.
This is the glorious victory they won.
But we—we Trojans died to save our people.
Oh, fly from war if you are wise. But if war comes,
to die well is to win the victor's crown."

But many whom war kills cannot win that crown.
The women talk little about the heroes, much about
the helpless. They think of the children who are

Crying, crying,
calling to us with tears,
Mother, I am all alone—

They see the capture of the city through their eyes;
the terrible moment of the Greeks' entry as childish
ears heard it:

A shout rang out in the town,
a cry of blood through the houses,
and a frightened child caught his mother's skirt
and hid himself in her cloak,
while War came forth from his hiding place.

A child's death is the chief action in this play about
war. A little boy, hardly grown beyond babyhood,
is taken from his mother by the Greeks to be killed.

She holds him in her arms and talks to him. She bids
him:

> Go die, my best-beloved, my own, my treasure,
> in cruel hands.
> Weeping, my little one? There, there,
> you cannot know. You little thing
> curled in my arms, how sweet the fragrance of you—
> Kiss me. Never again. Come closer, closer—
> Your mother who bore you—put your arms around
>   her neck.
> Now kiss me, lips to lips—

When the little dead body is brought back, the
mother is gone, hurried away to a Greek ship. Only
the grandmother is there to receive it. She holds his
hands,

> Dear hands, the same dear shape your father's had,
> how loosely now you fall. And dear proud lips
> forever closed.

She remembers the small boy climbing on to her bed
in the morning and telling her what he would do
when he was grown up.

> Not you, but I, old, homeless, childless,
> must lay you in your grave, so young,
> so miserably dead.

"The poet of the world's grief," Euripides was
called: in this play about war he sounded the deepest depths of that grief. How not, he would have
said, since no other suffering approaches that which
war inflicts.

IV

THE TROJAN WOMEN
of EURIPIDES

ꞁꞁꞁ

(*The scene is a space of waste ground except for a few huts to right and left, where the women selected for the Greek leaders are housed. Far in the background Troy, the wall in ruins, is slowly burning, as yet more smoke than flame. In front a woman with white hair lies on the ground. It is just before dawn. A tall dim figure is seen, back of the woman.*)

POSEIDON

I am the sea god. I have come
up from the salt sea depths of the Aegean,
from where the sea nymphs' footsteps fall,
weaving the lovely measures of the dance.
For since that day I built the towers of stone
around this town of Troy, Apollo with me,
—and straight we raised them, true by line and plummet—
good will for them has never left my heart,

my Trojans and their city.
City? Smoke only—all is gone,
perished beneath Greek spears.
A horse was fashioned, big with arms.
Parnassus was the workman's home,
in Phocia, and his name Epeius.
The skill he had Athena gave him.
He sent it through the walls—it carried death.
The wooden horse, so men will call it always,
which held and hid those spears.
A desert now where groves were. Blood drips down
from the gods' shrines. Beside his hearth
Priam lies dead upon the altar steps
of Zeus, the hearth's protector.
While to the Greek ships pass the Trojan treasure,
gold, gold in masses, armor, clothing,
stripped from the dead.
The Greeks who long since brought war to the
        town,
—ten times the seed was sown before Troy fell—
wait now for a fair wind for home,
the joyful sight of wife and child again.
Myself defeated by the Argive goddess
Hera and by Athena, both in league together—
I too must take my leave of glorious Troy,
forsake my altars. When a town is turned
into a desert, things divine fall sick.
Not one to do them honor.
Scamander's stream is loud with lamentation,
so many captive women weeping.
Their masters drew lots for them. Some will go
to Arcady and some to Thessaly.

Some to the lords of Athens, Theseus' sons.
Huts here hold others spared the lot, but chosen
for the great captains.
With them, like them a captive of the spear,
the Spartan woman, Helen.
But if a man would look on misery,
it is here to see—Hecuba lies there
before the gates. She weeps.
Many tears for many griefs.
And one still hidden from her.
But now upon Achilles' grave her daughter
was killed—Polyxena. So patiently she died.
Gone is her husband, gone her sons, all dead.
One daughter whom the Lord Apollo loved,
yet spared her wild virginity, Cassandra,
Agamemnon, in the dark, will force upon his bed.
No thought for what was holy and was God's.
O city happy once, farewell.
O shining towers, crumbling now
beneath Athena's hand, the child of God,
or you would still stand firm on deep foundations.

(*As he turns to go the goddess* PALLAS ATHENA *enters.*)

ATHENA

Am I allowed to speak to one who is
my father's nearest kinsman,
a god among gods honored, powerful?
If I put enmity aside, will he?

POSEIDON

He will, most high Athena. We are kin,
old comrades too, and these have magic power.

ATHENA

Thanks for your gentleness. What I would say
touches us both, great king.

POSEIDON

A message from the gods? A word from Zeus?
Some spirit, surely?

ATHENA

No, but for Troy's sake, where we stand, I seek
your power to join my own with it.

POSEIDON

What! Now—at last? Has that long hatred left you?
Pity—when all is ashes—burned to ashes?

ATHENA

The point first, please. Will you make common
    cause
with me? What I wish done will you wish, too?

POSEIDON

Gladly. But what you wish I first must know.
You come to me for Troy's sake or for Greece?

ATHENA

I wish to make my Trojan foes rejoice,
and give the Greeks a bitter home-coming. ╱

POSEIDON

The way you change! Here—there—then back again.
Now hate, now love—no limit ever.

ATHENA

You know how I was outraged and my temple.

POSEIDON

Oh that—when Ajax dragged Cassandra out?

ATHENA

And not one Greek to punish him—not one to blame
him.

POSEIDON

Even though your power ruined Troy for them.

ATHENA

Therefore with you I mean to hurt them.

POSEIDON

Ready for all you wish. But—hurt them? How?

ATHENA

Give them affliction for their coming home.

POSEIDON

Held here, you mean? Or out on the salt sea?

ATHENA

Whenever the ships sail.
Zeus shall send rain, unending rain, and sleet,
and darkness blown from heaven.
He will give me—he has promised—his thunderbolt,
to strike the ships with fire. They shall burn.
Your part, to make your sea-roads roar—
wild waves and whirlwinds,
while dead men choke the winding bay.
So Greeks shall learn to reverence my house
and dread all gods.

POSEIDON

These things shall be. No need of many words
to grant a favor. I will stir the sea,

the wide Aegean. Shores and reefs and cliffs
will hold dead men, bodies of many dead.
Off to Olympus with you now, and get
those fiery arrows from the hand of Zeus.
Then when a fair wind sends the Greeks to sea,
watch the ships sail.
    (*Exit* ATHENA.)
Oh, fools, the men who lay a city waste,
giving to desolation temples, tombs,
the sanctuaries of the dead—so soon
to die themselves.
    (*Exit* POSEIDON.)
    (*The two gods have been talking before daylight,
    but now the day begins to dawn and the woman
    lying on the ground in front moves. She is* HECUBA,
    the aged queen of Troy.)

HECUBA

Up from the ground—O weary head, O breaking
    neck.
This is no longer Troy. And we are not
the lords of Troy.
Endure. The ways of fate are the ways of the wind.
Drift with the stream—drift with fate.
No use to turn the prow to breast the waves.
Let the boat go as it chances.
Sorrow, my sorrow.
What sorrow is there that is not mine,
grief to weep for.
Country lost and children and husband.
Glory of all my house brought low.
All was nothing—nothing, always.

Keep silent? Speak?
Weep then? Why? For what?
　(*She begins to get up.*)
Oh, this aching body—this bed—
it is very hard. My back pressed to it—
Oh, my side, my brow, my temples.
Up! Quick, quick. I must move.
Oh, I'll rock myself this way, that way,
to the sound of weeping, the song of tears,
dropping down forever.
The song no feet will dance to ever,
for the wretched, the ruined.

O ships, O prows, swift oars,
out from the fair Greek bays and harbors,
over the dark shining sea,
you found your way to our holy city,
and the fearful music of war was heard,
the war song sung to flute and pipe,
as you cast on the shore your cables,
ropes the Nile dwellers twisted and coiled,
and you swung, oh, my grief, in Troy's waters.

What did you come for? A woman?
A thing of loathing, of shame,
to husband, to brother, to home.
She slew Priam, the king,
father of fifty sons,
she wrecked me upon
the reef of destruction.

Who am I that I wait *
here at a Greek king's door?
A slave that men drive on,
an old gray woman that has no home.
Shaven head brought low in dishonor.
O wives of the bronze-armored men who fought,
and maidens, sorrowing maidens,
plighted to shame,
see—only smoke left where was Troy.
Let us weep for her.
As a mother bird cries to her feathered brood,
so will I cry.
Once another song I sang
when I leaned on Priam's scepter,
and the beat of dancing feet
marked the music's measure.
Up to the gods
the song of Troy rose at my signal.

*(The door of one of the huts opens and a woman
steals out, then another, and another.)*

FIRST WOMAN

Your cry, O Hecuba—oh, such a cry—
What does it mean? There in the tent
we heard you call so piteously,
and through our hearts flashed fear.
In the tent we were weeping, too,
for we are slaves.

HECUBA

Look, child, there where the Greek ships lie—

* This is the way Professor Murray translates the line and the
one following. The translation is so simple and beautiful, I cannot bear to give it up for a poorer one of my own.

ANOTHER WOMAN

They are moving. The men hold oars.

ANOTHER

O God, what will they do? Carry me off
over the sea in a ship far from home?

HECUBA

You ask and I know nothing,
but I think ruin is here.

ANOTHER WOMAN

Oh, we are wretched. We shall hear the summons.
Women of Troy, go forth from your home,
for the Greeks set sail.

HECUBA

But not Cassandra, oh, not her.
She is mad—she has been driven mad. Leave her
    within.
Not shamed before the Greeks—not that grief too.
I have enough.
    O Troy, unhappy Troy, you are gone
and we, the unhappy, leave you,
we who are living and we who are dead.
    (*More women now come out from a second hut.*)

A WOMAN

Out of the Greek king's tent
trembling I come, O Queen,
to hear my fate from you.
Not death— They would not think of death
for a poor woman.

ANOTHER

The sailors—they are standing on the prow.
Already they are running out the oars.

ANOTHER

(*she comes out of a third hut and several follow her.*)
It is so early—but a terror woke me.
    My heart beats so.

ANOTHER

Has a herald come from the Greek camp?
Whose slave shall I be? I—bear that?

HECUBA

Wait for the lot drawing. It is near.

ANOTHER

Argos shall it be, or Phthia?
    or an island of the sea?
    A Greek soldier lead me there,
far, far from Troy?

HECUBA

And I a slave—to whom—where—how?
You old gray woman, patient to endure,
you bee without a sting,
only an image of what was alive.
    or the ghost of one dead.
I watch a master's door?
    I nurse his children?
    Once I was queen in Troy.

ONE WOMAN TO ANOTHER

Poor thing. What are your tears
to the shame before you?

THE OTHER

The shuttle will still pass through my hands,
    but the loom will not be in Troy.

ANOTHER

My dead sons. I would look at them once more.
Never again.

ANOTHER

Worse to come.
A Greek's bed—and I—

ANOTHER

A night like that? Oh, never—
    oh, no—not that for me.

ANOTHER

I see myself a water carrier,
dipping my pitcher in the great Pierian spring.

ANOTHER

The land of Theseus, Athens, it is known
to be a happy place. I wish I could go there.

ANOTHER

But not to the Eurotas, hateful river,
where Helen lived. Not there, to be a slave
to Menelaus who sacked Troy.

ANOTHER

Oh, look. A man from the Greek army—
a herald. Something strange has happened,
he comes so fast. To tell us—what?
What will he say? Only Greek slaves are here,
waiting for orders.
    (*Enter* TALTHYBIUS *with soldiers.*)

TALTHYBIUS

You know me, Hecuba. I have often come
with messages to Troy from the Greek camp.
Talthybius—these many years you've known me.
I bring you news.

HECUBA

It has come, women of Troy. Once we only feared it.

TALTHYBIUS

The lots are drawn, if that is what you feared.

HECUBA

Who—where? Thessaly? Phthia? Thebes?

TALTHYBIUS

A different man takes each. You're not to go together.

HECUBA

Then which takes which? Has any one good fortune?

TALTHYBIUS

I know, but ask about each one, not all at once.

HECUBA

My daughter, who—who drew her? Tell me—
Cassandra. She has had so much to bear.

TALTHYBIUS

King Agamemnon chose her out from all.

HECUBA

Oh! but—of course—to serve his Spartan wife?

TALTHYBIUS

No, no—but for the king's own bed at night.

HECUBA

Oh, never. She is God's, a virgin, always.
That was God's gift to her for all her life.

TALTHYBIUS

He loved her for that same strange purity.*

HECUBA

Throw away, daughter, the keys of the temple.
Take off the wreath and the sacred stole.

TALTHYBIUS

Well, now—a king's bed is not so bad.

HECUBA

My other child you took from me just now?

TALTHYBIUS
(*speaking with constraint.*)
Polyxena, you mean? Or someone else?

HECUBA

Her. Who drew her?

TALTHYBIUS

They told her off to watch Achilles' tomb.

HECUBA

To watch a tomb? My daughter?
That a Greek custom?
What strange ritual is that, my friend?

TALTHYBIUS
(*speaking fast and trying to put her off.*)
Just think of her as happy—all well with her.

* This line, too, is Professor Murray's, and retained here for
the reason given above.

HECUBA

Those words— Why do you speak like that?
She is alive?

TALTHYBIUS

(*determined not to tell her.*)
What happened was—well, she is free from trouble.

HECUBA

(*wearily giving the riddle up.*)
Then Hector's wife—my Hector, wise in war—
Where does she go, poor thing—Andromache?

TALTHYBIUS

Achilles' son took her. He chose her out.

HECUBA

And I, old gray head, whose slave am I,
creeping along with my crutch?

TALTHYBIUS

Slave of the king of Ithaca, Odysseus.

HECUBA

Beat, beat my shorn head! Tear, tear my cheek!
His slave—vile lying man. I have come to this—
There is nothing good he does not hurt—a lawless
    beast.
He twists and turns, this way and that, and back
    again.
A double tongue, as false in hate as false in love.
Pity me, women of Troy,
I have gone. I am lost—oh, wretched.
An evil fate fell on me,
a lot the hardest of all.

A WOMAN

You know what lies before you, Queen, but I—
What man among the Greeks owns me?

TALTHYBIUS *(to the soldiers.)*

Off with you. Bring Cassandra here. Be quick,
you fellows. We must give her to the chief,
into his very hand. And then these here
to all the other generals. But what's that—
that flash of light inside there?

    (*Light shines through the crevices of one of the huts.*)

Set fire to the huts—is that their plan,
these Trojan women? Burn themselves to death
rather than sail to Greece. Choosing to die instead.
How savagely these days the yoke bears down
on necks so lately free.

Open there, open the door. (*Aside.*) As well for
    them perhaps,
but for the Greeks—they'd put the blame on me.

HECUBA

No, no, there is nothing burning. It is my daughter,
Cassandra. She is mad.

    (CASSANDRA *enters from the hut dressed like a priestess, a wreath in her hair, a torch in her hand. She does not seem to see anyone.*)

CASSANDRA

Lift it high—in my hand—light to bring.
  I praise him. I bear a flame.
  With my torch I touch to fire
  this holy place.

Hymen, O Hymen.
Blessed the bridegroom,
blessed am I
to lie with a king in a king's bed in Argos.
Hymen, O Hymen.
Mother, you weep
tears for my father dead,
mourning for the beloved
country lost.
I for my bridal here
lift up the fire's flame
to the dawn, to the splendor,
to you, O Hymen.
Queen of night,
give your starlight
to a virgin bed,
as of old you did.
Fly, dancing feet.
Up with the dance.
Oh, joy, oh, joy!
Dance for my father dead,
most blest to die.
Oh, holy dance!
Apollo—you?
Lead on then.
There in the laurel grove
I served your altar.
Dance, Mother, come.
Keep step with me.
Dear feet with my feet
tracing the measure
this way and that.

Sing to the Marriage god,
oh, joyful song.
Sing for the bride, too,
joyously all.
Maidens of Troy,
dressed in your best,
honor my marriage.
Honor too him
whose bed fate drives me to share.

A WOMAN

Hold her fast, Queen, poor frenzied girl.
She might rush straight to the Greek camp.

HECUBA

O fire, fire, when men make marriages
you light the torch, but this flame flashing here
is for grief only. Child, such great hopes once I had.
I never thought that to your bridal bed
Greek spears would drive you.
Give me your torch. You do not hold it straight,
you move so wildly. Your sufferings, my child,
have never taught you wisdom.
You never change. Here! someone take the torch
into the hut. This marriage needs no songs,
but only tears.

CASSANDRA

O Mother, crown my triumph with a wreath.
Be glad, for I am married to a king.
Send me to him, and if I shrink away,
drive me with violence. If Apollo lives,
my marriage shall be bloodier than Helen's.

Agamemnon, the great, the glorious lord of Greece—
I shall kill him, Mother, lay his house as low
as he laid ours, make him pay for all
he made my father suffer, brothers, and—
But no. I must not speak of that—that axe
which on my neck—on others' too—
nor of that murder of a mother.
All, all because he married me and so
pulled his own house down.
But I will show you. This town now, yes, Mother,
is happier than the Greeks. I know that I am mad,
but Mother, dearest, now, for this one time
I do not rave.
One woman they came hunting, and one love,
Helen, and men by tens of thousands died.
Their king, so wise, to get what most he hated
destroyed what most he loved,
his joy at home, his daughter, killing her
for a brother's sake, to get him back a woman
who had fled because she wished—not forced to go.
And when they came to the banks of the Scamander
those thousands died. And why?
No man had moved their landmarks
or laid siege to their high-walled towns.
But those whom war took never saw their children.
No wife with gentle hands shrouded them for their
          grave.
They lie in a strange land. And in their homes
are sorrows, too, the very same.
Lonely women who died, old men who waited
for sons that never came—no son left to them
to make the offering at their graves.

That was the glorious victory they won.
But we—we Trojans died to save our people,
no glory greater. All those the spear slew,
friends bore them home and wrapped them in their
    shroud
with dutiful hands. The earth of their own land
covered them. The rest, through the long days they
    fought,
had wife and child at hand, not like the Greeks,
whose joys were far away.
And Hector's pain—your Hector. Mother, hear me.
This is the truth: he died, the best, a hero.
Because the Greeks came, he died thus.
Had they stayed home, we never would have known
    him.
This truth stands firm: the wise will fly from war.
But if war comes, to die well is to win
the victor's crown.
The only shame is not to die like that.
So, Mother, do not pity Troy,
or me upon my bridal bed.

TALTHYBIUS

(*has been held awestruck through all this, but can
    bear no more.*)
Now if Apollo had not made you mad
I would have paid you for those evil words,
bad omens, and my general sailing soon.
    (*Grumbles to himself.*)
The great, who seem so wise, have no more sense
than those who rank as nothing.
Our king, the first in Greece, bows down

before this mad girl, loves her, chooses her
out of them all. Well, I am a poor man,
but I'd not go to bed with her.
   (*Turns to* CASSANDRA.)
Now you—you know your mind is not quite right.
So all you said against Greece and for Troy,
I never heard—the wind blew it away.
Come with me to the ship now.
   (*Aside.*)
A grand match for our general, she is.
   (*To* HECUBA, *gently.*)
And you, do follow quietly when Odysseus' men
      come.
His wife's a good, wise woman, so they say.

CASSANDRA

(*seeming to see* TALTHYBIUS *for the first time and
            looking him over haughtily.*)
A strange sort of slave, surely.
Heralds such men are called,
hated by all, for they are tyrants' tools.
You say my mother goes to serve Odysseus?
   (*She turns away and speaks to herself.*)
But where then is Apollo's word, made clear
to me, that death will find her here?
And—no, that shame I will not speak of.
Odysseus! wretched—but he does not know.
   Soon all these sorrows, mine and Troy's, will seem
compared to his like golden hours.
Ten years behind him here, ten years before him.
Then only, all alone, will he come home,
and there find untold trouble has come first.

But his cares—why let fly one word at him?
Come, let us hasten to my marriage.
We two shall rest, the bridegroom and the bride,
within the house of death.
O Greek king, with your dreams of grandeur yet to
    come,
vile as you are, so shall your end be,
in darkness—all light gone.
And me—a cleft in the hills,
washed by winter rains,
his tomb near by.
There—dead—cast out—naked—
and wild beasts seeking food—
It is I there—I myself—Apollo's servant.
O flowers of the God I love, mysterious wreaths,
away. I have forgotten temple festival,
I have forgotten joy.
Off. I tear them from my neck.
Swift winds will carry them
up to you, O God of truth.
My flesh still clean, I give them back to you.
Where is the ship? How do I go on board?
Spread the sail—the wind comes swift.
Those who bring vengeance—three are they,
And one of them goes with you on the sea.
Mother, my Mother, do not weep. Farewell,
dear City. Brothers, in Troy's earth laid, my father,
a little time and I am with you.
You dead, I shall come to you a victor.
Those ruined by my hand who ruined us.

　　(*She goes out with* TALTHYBIUS *and the soldiers.*
　　HECUBA, *motionless for a moment, falls.*)

A WOMAN

The Queen! See—see—she is falling.
Oh, help! She cannot speak.
Miserable slaves, will you leave her on the ground,
old as she is. Up—lift her up.

HECUBA

Let me be. Kindness not wanted is unkindness.
I cannot stand. Too much is on me.
Anguish here and long since and to come—
O God— Do I call to you? You did not help.
But there is something that cries out for God
when trouble comes.
Oh, I will think of good days gone,
days to make a song of,
crowning my sorrow by remembering.
We were kings and a king I married.
Sons I bore him, many sons.
That means little—but fine, brave lads.
They were the best in all Troy.
No woman, Trojan, Greek, or stranger,
had sons like mine to be proud of.
I saw them fall beneath Greek spears.
My hair I shore at the grave of the dead.
Their father—I did not learn from others
that I must weep for him—these eyes beheld him.
I, my own self, saw him fall murdered
upon the altar, when his town was lost.
My daughters, maidens reared to marry kings,
are torn from me. For the Greeks I reared them.
All gone—no hope that I shall look upon
their faces any more, or they on mine.

And now the end—no more can lie beyond—
an old gray slave woman I go to Greece.
The tasks they know for my age hardest, mine.
The door to shut and open, bowing low
—I who bore Hector—meal to grind; upon
the ground lay this old body down that once
slept in a royal bed; torn rags around me,
torn flesh beneath.
And all this misery and all to come
because a man desired a woman.
Daughter, who knew God's mystery and joy,
what strange chance lost you your virginity?
And you, Polyxena—where are you gone?
No son, no daughter, left to help my need,
and I had many, many—
Why lift me up? What hope is there to hold to?
    This slave that once went delicately in Troy,
take her and cast her on her bed of clay,
rocks for her pillow, there to fall and die,
wasted with tears. Count no one happy,
however fortunate, before he dies.

CHORUS

Sing me, O Muse, a song for Troy,
a strange song sung to tears,
a music for the grave.
O lips, sound forth a melody
    for Troy.

A four-wheeled cart brought the horse to the gates,
brought ruin to me,
    captured, enslaved me.
Gold was the rein and the bridle,

deadly the arms within,
and they clashed loud to heaven as the threshold was
     passed.

High on Troy's rock the people cried,
"Rest at last, trouble ended.
Bring the carven image in.
Bear it to Athena,
fit gift for the child of God."

Who of the young but hurried forth?
Who of the old would stay at home?
With song and rejoicing they brought death in,
treachery and destruction.

All that were in Troy,
hastening to the gate,
drew that smooth-planed horse of wood
carven from a mountain pine,
where the Greeks were hiding,
where was Troy's destruction,
gave it to the goddess,
gift for her, the virgin,
driver of the steeds that never die.

With ropes of twisted flax,
as a ship's dark hull is drawn to land,
they brought it to her temple of stone,
to her floor that soon would run with blood,
     to Pallas Athena.

     On their toil and their joy
the dark of evening fell,
but the lutes of Egypt still rang out
     to the songs of Troy.

And girls with feet light as air
dancing, sang happy songs.
The houses blazed with light
through the dark splendor,
    and sleep was not.

A GIRL

I was among the dancers.
I was singing to the maiden of Zeus,
the goddess of the hills.
A shout rang out in the town,
a cry of blood through the houses,
and a frightened child caught his mother's skirt
and hid himself in her cloak.
Then War came forth from his hiding place—
Athena, the virgin, devised it.
Around the altars they slaughtered us.
Within on their beds lay headless men,
young men cut down in their prime.
This was the triumph-crown of Greece.
We shall bear children for her to rear,
grief and shame to our country.
    (*A chariot approaches, loaded with spoils. In it sits
    a woman and a child.*)

A WOMAN

Look, Hecuba, it is Andromache.
See, in the Greek car yonder.
Her breast heaves with her sobs and yet
the baby sleeps there, dear Astyanax,
    the son of Hector.

ANOTHER

Most sorrowful of women, where do you go?
Beside you the bronze armor that was Hector's,
the spoil of the Greek spear, stripped from the dead.
Will Achilles' son use it to deck his temples?

ANDROMACHE

I go where my Greek masters take me.

HECUBA

Oh, our sorrow—our sorrow.

ANDROMACHE

Why should you weep? This sorrow is mine.

HECUBA

O God—

ANDROMACHE

What has come to me is mine.

HECUBA

My children—

ANDROMACHE

Once we lived, not now.

HECUBA

Gone—gone—happiness—Troy—

ANDROMACHE

And you bear it.

HECUBA

Sons, noble sons, all lost.

ANDROMACHE

Oh, sorrow is here.

HECUBA

For me—for me.

ANDROMACHE

For the city, in its shroud of smoke.
Come to me, O my husband.

HECUBA

What you cry to lies in the grave.
My son, wretched woman, mine.

ANDROMACHE

Defend me—me, your wife.

HECUBA

My son, my eldest son,
whom I bore to Priam,
whom the Greeks used shamefully,
come to me, lead me to death.

ANDROMACHE

Death—oh, how deep a desire.

HECUBA

Such is our pain—

ANDROMACHE

For a city that has fallen, fallen.

HECUBA

For anguish heaped upon anguish.

ANDROMACHE

For the anger of God against Paris,
your son, who fled from death,
who laid Troy's towers low
to win an evil love.

Dead men—bodies—blood—
vultures hovering—
Oh, Athena the goddess is there, be sure,
and the slave's yoke is laid upon Troy.

HECUBA

O country, desolate, empty.

ANDROMACHE

My tears fall for you.

HECUBA

Look and see the end—

ANDROMACHE

Of the house where I bore my children.

HECUBA

O children, your mother has lost her city,
and you—you have left her alone.
Only grief is mine and mourning.
Tears and more tears, falling, falling.
The dead—they have forgotten their pain.
They weep no more.

A WOMAN (*aside to another.*)

Tears are sweet in bitter grief,
and sorrow's song is lamentation.

ANDROMACHE

Mother of him whose spear of old brought death
to Greeks unnumbered, you see what is here.

HECUBA

I see God's hand that casts the mighty down
and sets on high the lowly.

ANDROMACHE

Driven like cattle captured in a raid,
my child and I—the free changed to a slave.
Oh, changed indeed.

HECUBA

It is fearful to be helpless. Men just now
have taken Cassandra—forced her from me.

ANDROMACHE

And still more for you—more than that—

HECUBA

Number my sorrows, will you? Measure them?
One comes—the next one rivals it.

ANDROMACHE

Polyxena lies dead upon Achilles' tomb,
a gift to a corpse, to a lifeless thing.

HECUBA

My sorrow! That is what Talthybius meant—
I could not read his riddle. Oh, too plain.

ANDROMACHE

I saw her there and left the chariot
and covered her dead body with my cloak,
and beat my breast.

HECUBA

Murdered—my child. Oh, wickedly!
Again I cry to you. Oh, cruelly slain!

ANDROMACHE

She has died her death, and happier by far
dying than I alive.

HECUBA

Life cannot be what death is, child.
Death is empty—life has hope.

ANDROMACHE

Mother, O Mother, hear a truer word.
Now let me bring joy to your heart.
I say to die is only not to be,
and rather death than life with bitter grief.
They have no pain, they do not feel their wrongs.
But the happy who has come to wretchedness,
his soul is a lost wanderer,
the old joys that were once, left far behind.
She is dead, your daughter—to her the same
as if she never had been born.
She does not know the wickedness that killed her.
While I—I aimed my shaft at good repute.
I gained full measure—then missed happiness.
For all that is called virtuous in a woman
I strove for and I won in Hector's house.
Always, because we women, whether right or
    wrong,
are spoken ill of
unless we stay within our homes, my longing
I set aside and kept the house.
Light talk, glib women's words,
could never gain an entrance there.
My own thoughts were enough for me,
best of all teachers to me in my home.
Silence, a tranquil eye, I brought my husband,

knew well in what I should rule him,
and when give him obedience.
And this report of me came to the Greeks
for my destruction. When they captured me
Achilles' son would have me.
I shall be a slave to those who murdered—
O Hector, my beloved—shall I thrust him aside,
open my heart to the man that comes to me,
and be a traitor to the dead?
And yet to shrink in loathing from him
and make my masters hate me—
One night, men say, one night in a man's bed
will make a woman tame—
Oh, shame! A woman throw her husband off
and in a new bed love another—
Why, a young colt will not run in the yoke
with any but her mate—not a dumb beast
that has no reason, of a lower nature.
O Hector, my beloved, you were all to me,
wise, noble, mighty, in wealth, in manhood, both.
No man had touched me when you took me,
took me from out my father's home
and yoked a girl fast to you.
And you are dead, and I, with other plunder,
am sent by sea to Greece. A slave's yoke there.
Your dead Polyxena you weep for,
what does she know of pain like mine?
The living must have hope. Not I, not any more.
I will not lie to my own heart. No good will ever
    come.
But oh, to think it would be sweet.

A WOMAN

We stand at the same point of pain. You mourn your
        ruin,
and in your words I hear my own calamity.

HECUBA

Those ships—I never have set foot on one,
but I have heard of them, seen pictures of them.
I know that when a storm comes which they think
they can ride out, the sailors do their best,
one by the sail, another at the helm,
and others bailing.
But if great ocean's raging overwhelms them,
they yield to fate.
They give themselves up to the racing waves.
So in my many sorrows I am dumb.
I yield, I cannot speak.
The great wave from God has conquered me.
But, O dear child, let Hector be,
and let be what has come to him.
Your tears will never call him back.
Give honor now to him who is your master.
Your sweet ways—use them to allure him.
So doing you will give cheer to your friends.
Perhaps this child, my own child's son,
you may rear to manhood and great aid for Troy,
and if ever you should have more children,
they might build her again. Troy once more be a
        city!
Oh—one thought leads another on.
But why again that servant of the Greeks?

I see him coming. Some new plan is here.
  (*Enter* TALTHYBIUS *with soldiers. He is troubled
  and advances hesitatingly.*)

TALTHYBIUS

Wife of the noblest man that was in Troy,
O wife of Hector, do not hate me.
Against my will I come to tell you.
The people and the kings have all resolved—

ANDROMACHE

What is it? Evil follows words like those.

TALTHYBIUS

This child they order— Oh, how can I say it—

ANDROMACHE

Not that he does not go with me to the same master—

TALTHYBIUS

No man in Greece shall ever be his master.

ANDROMACHE

But—leave him here—all that is left of Troy?

TALTHYBIUS

I don't know how to tell you. What is bad,
words can't make better—

ANDROMACHE

I feel you kind. But you have not good news.

TALTHYBIUS

Your child must die. There, now you know
the whole, bad as it is.

ANDROMACHE

Oh, I have heard an evil worse
than a slave in her master's bed.

TALTHYBIUS

It was Odysseus had his way. He spoke
to all the Greeks.

ANDROMACHE

O God. There is no measure to my pain.

TALTHYBIUS

He said a hero's son must not grow up—

ANDROMACHE

God, on his own sons may that counsel fall.

TALTHYBIUS

—but from the towering wall of Troy be thrown.
Now, now— let it be done— that's wiser.
Don't cling so to him. Bear your pain
the way a brave woman suffers.
You have no strength—don't look to any help.
There's no help for you anywhere. Think—think.
The city gone—your husband too. And you
a captive and alone, one woman—how
can you do battle with us? For your own good
I would not have you try, and draw
hatred down on you and be shamed.
Oh, hush—never a curse upon the Greeks.
If you say words that make the army angry
the child will have no burial, and without pity—
Silence now. Bear your fate as best you can.
So then you need not leave him dead without a grave,
and you will find the Greeks more kind.

ANDROMACHE

Go die, my best beloved, my own, my treasure,
in cruel hands, leaving your mother comfortless.
Your father was too noble. That is why
they kill you. He could save others,
he could not save you for his nobleness.
My bed, my bridal—all for misery—
when long ago I came to Hector's halls
to bear my son—oh, not for Greeks to slay,
but for a ruler over teeming Asia.
Weeping, my little one? There, there.
You cannot know what waits for you.
Why hold me with your hands so fast, cling so fast
    to me?
You little bird, flying to hide beneath my wings.
And Hector will not come—he will not come,
up from the tomb, great spear in hand. to save you.
Not one of all his kin, of all the Trojan might.
How will it be? Falling down—down—oh, horrible.
And his neck—his breath—all broken.
And none to pity. You little thing,
curled in my arms, you dearest to your mother,
how sweet the fragrance of you.
All nothing then—this breast from where
your baby mouth drew milk, my travail too,
my cares, when I grew wasted watching you.
Kiss me— Never again. Come, closer, closer.
Your mother who bore you—put your arms around
    my neck.
Now kiss me, lips to lips.
O Greeks, you have found out ways to torture

that are not Greek.
A little child, all innocent of wrong—
you wish to kill him.
O Helen, evil growth, that was sown by Tyndareus,
you are no child of Zeus, as people say.
Many the fathers you were born of,
Madness, Hatred, Red Death, whatever poison
the earth brings forth—no child of Zeus,
but Greece's curse and all the world's.
God curse you, with those beautiful eyes
that brought to shame and ruin
Troy's far-famed plains.
Quick! take him—seize him—cast him down—
if so you will. Feast on his flesh.
God has destroyed me, and I cannot—
I cannot save my child from death.
Oh hide my head for shame and fling me
into the ship.

    (*She falls, then struggles to her knees.*)
My fair bridal—I am coming—
Oh, I have lost my child, my own.

A WOMAN

O wretched Troy, tens of thousands lost
for a woman's sake, a hateful marriage bed.

TALTHYBIUS (*drawing the child away.*)
Come, boy, let go. Unclasp those loving hands,
poor mother.
Come now, up, up, to the very height,
where the towers of your fathers crown the wall,
and where it is decreed that you must die.

(To the soldiers.)
Take him away.
A herald who must bring such orders
should be a man who feels no pity,
and no shame either—not like me.

HECUBA

Child, son of my poor son, whose toil was all in vain,
we are robbed, your mother and I, oh, cruelly—
robbed of your life. How bear it?
What can I do for you, poor piteous child?
Beat my head, my breast—all I can give you.
Troy lost, now you—all lost.
The cup is full. Why wait? For what?
Hasten on—swiftly on to death.

> *(The soldiers, who have waited while* HECUBA *speaks, go out with the child and* TALTHYBIUS. *One of them takes* ANDROMACHE *to the chariot and drives off with her.)*

CHORUS

The waves make a ring around Salamis.
The bees are loud in the island.
King Telamon built him a dwelling.
It fronted the holy hills,
where first the gray gleaming olive
Athena showed to men,
the glory of shining Athens,
her crown from the sky.
He joined himself to the bowman,
the son of Alcmena, for valorous deeds.
Troy, Troy he laid waste, my city,
long ago when he went forth from Greece.

When he led forth from Greece the bravest
in his wrath for the steeds * withheld,
and by fair-flowing Simois stayed his oar
that had brought him over the sea.
Cables there made the ship fast.
In his hand was the bow that never missed.
It brought the king to his death.
Walls of stone that Phoebus had built
he wrecked with the red breath of fire.
He wasted the plain of Troy.
Twice her walls have fallen. Twice
a blood-stained spear struck her down,
      laid her in ruin.

In vain, O you who move
with delicate feet where the wine-cups are gold,
son of that old dead king,
who fill with wine the cup Zeus holds,
service most fair—
she who gave you birth is afire.
The shores of the sea are wailing for her.
As a bird cries over her young,
women weep for husbands, for children,
for the old, too, who gave them birth.
Your dewy baths are gone,
and the race-course where you ran.
Yet your young face keeps the beauty of peace
in joy, by the throne of Zeus.

---

* When Troy was destroyed the first time, the reason was
that the Trojan king had promised two immortal horses to
Hercules ("the son of Alcmena") but did not give them to him.
Hercules in revenge ruined the city. The son of this king was
Ganymede, cup-bearer to Zeus.

While Priam's land
lies ruined by Greek spearsmen.

Love, O Love,
once you came to the halls of Troy,
and your song rose up to the dwellers in heaven.
How did you then exalt Troy high,
binding her fast to the gods, by a union—
No—I will not speak blame of Zeus.
But the light of white-winged Dawn, dear to men,
is deadly over the land this day,
shining on fallen towers.
And yet Dawn keeps in her bridal bower
her children's father, a son of Troy.
Her chariot bore him away to the sky.
It was gold, and four stars drew it.
Hope was high then for our town.
But the magic that brought her the love of the gods
has gone from Troy.
   (*As the song ends* MENELAUS *enters with a body-
   guard of soldiers.*)

MENELAUS

How bright the sunlight is today—
this day, when I shall get into my power
Helen, my wife. For I am Menelaus,
the man of many wrongs.
I came to Troy and brought with me my army,
not for that woman's sake, as people say,
but for the man who from my house,
and he a guest there, stole away my wife.
Ah, well, with God's help he has paid the price,

he and his country, fallen beneath Greek spears.
I am come to get her—wretch—I cannot speak her
    name
who was my wife once.
In a hut here, where they house the captives,
she is numbered with the other Trojan women.
The men who fought and toiled to win her back,
have given her to me—to kill, or else,
if it pleases me, to take her back to Argos.
And it has seemed to me her death in Troy
is not the way. I will take her overseas,
with swift oars speeding on the ship,
and there in Greece give her to those to kill
whose dearest died because of her.
    (*To his men.*)
Attention! Forward to the huts.
Seize her and drag her out by that long blood-
    drenched hair—
    (*Stops suddenly and controls himself.*)
And when fair winds come, home with her to
Greece.
    (*Soldiers begin to force the door of one of the
    huts.*)

HECUBA
    (*comes slowly forward.*)
O thou who dost uphold the world,
whose throne is high above the world,
thou, past our seeking hard to find, who art thou?
God, or Necessity of what must be,
or Reason of our reason?
Whate'er thou art, I pray to thee,

seeing the silent road by which
all mortal things are led by thee to justice.

MENELAUS

What have we here? A queer prayer that.

HECUBA

(*she comes still nearer to him and he recognizes her.*)
Kill her, Menelaus? You will? Oh, blessings on you!
But—shun her, do not look at her.
Desire for her will seize you, conquer you.
For through men's eyes she gets them in her power.
She ruins them and ruins cities too.
Fire comes from her to burn homes,
magic for death. I know her—so do you,
and all these who have suffered.

> (HELEN *enters from the hut. The soldiers do not
> touch her. She is very gentle and undisturbed.*)

HELEN

(*with sweet, injured dignity. angry at all.*)   Not
Menelaus, these things might well make a woman
        fear.
Your men with violence have driven me from my
        room,
have laid their hands upon me.
Of course I know—almost I know—you hate me,
but yet I ask you, what is your decision,
yours and the Greeks? Am I to live or not?

MENELAUS

Nothing more clear. Unanimous, in fact.
Not one who did not vote you should be given me,
whom you have wronged, to kill you.

HELEN

Am I allowed to speak against the charge?
To show you if I die that I shall die
most wronged and innocent?

MENELAUS

I have come to kill you, not to argue with you.

HECUBA

Oh, hear her. She must never die unheard.
Then, Menelaus, let me answer her.
The evil that she did in Troy, you do not know.
But I will tell the story. She will die.
She never can escape.

MENELAUS

That means delay. Still—if she wants to speak,
she can. I grant her this because of what you say,
not for her sake. She can be sure of that.

HELEN

And perhaps, no matter if you think I speak
the truth or not, you will not talk to me,
since you believe I am your enemy.
Still, I will try to answer what I think
you would say if you spoke your mind,
and my wrongs shall be heard as well as yours.
First: who began these evils? She, the day
when she gave birth to Paris. Who next was guilty?
The old king who decreed the child should live,
and ruined Troy and me—Paris, the hateful,
the firebrand.
What happened then? Listen and learn.
This Paris—he was made the judge for three,

all yoked together in a quarrel—goddesses.
Athena promised he should lead the Trojans
to victory and lay all Greece in ruins.
And Hera said if he thought her the fairest
she would make him lord of Europe and of Asia.
But Aphrodite—well, she praised my beauty—
astonishing, she said—and promised him
that she would give me to him if he judged
that she was loveliest. Then, see what happened.
She won, and so my bridal brought all Greece
great good. No strangers rule you,
no foreign spears, no tyrant.
Oh, it was well for Greece, but not for me,
sold for my beauty and reproached besides
when I deserved a crown.
But—to the point. Is that what you are thinking?
Why did I go—steal from your house in secret?
That man, Paris, or any name you like to call him,
his mother's curse—oh, when he came to me
a mighty goddess walked beside him.
And you, poor fool, you spread your sails for Crete,
left Sparta—left him in your house.
Ah well— Not you, but my own self I ask,
what was there in my heart that I went with him,
a strange man, and forgot my home and country?
Not I, but Aphrodite. Punish her,
be mightier than Zeus who rules
the other gods, but is her slave.
She is my absolution—
One thing with seeming justice you might say.
When Paris died and went down to the grave,
and when no god cared who was in my bed,

I should have left his house—gone to the Greeks.
Just what I tried to do—oh, many times.
I have witnesses—the men who kept the gates,
the watchmen on the walls. Not once, but often
they found me swinging from a parapet,
a rope around this body, stealthily
feeling my way down.
The Trojans then no longer wanted me,
but the man who next took me—and by force—
would never let me go.
My husband, must I die, and at your hands?
You think that right? Is that your justice?
I was forced—by violence. I lived a life
that had no joy, no triumph. In bitterness
I lived a slave.
Do you wish to set yourself above the gods?
Oh, stupid, senseless wish!

A WOMAN

O Queen, defend your children and your country.
Her soft persuasive words are deadly.
She speaks so fair and is so vile.
A fearful thing.

HECUBA

Her goddesses will fight on my side while
I show her for the liar that she is.
Not Hera, not virgin Athena, do I think
would ever stoop to folly great enough
to sell their cities. Hera sell her Argos,
Athena Athens, to be the Trojan's slave!
playing like silly children there on Ida,
and each one in her insolence demanding

the prize for beauty. Beauty—why was Hera
so hot for it? That she might get herself
a better mate than Zeus?
Athena—who so fled from marriage that she begged
one gift from Zeus, virginity.
But she would have the prize, you say. And why?
To help her hunt some god to marry her?
Never make gods out fools to whitewash your own
    evil.
No one with sense will listen to you.
And Aphrodite, did you say—who would not laugh?
—must take my son to Menelaus' house?
Why? Could she not stay quietly in heaven
and send you on—and all your town—to Troy?
My son was beautiful exceedingly.
You saw him—your own desire was enough.
No need of any goddess.
Men's follies—they are Aphrodite.
She rose up from the sea-foam; where the froth
and foam of life are, there she is.
It was my son. You saw him in his Eastern dress
all bright with gold, and you were mad with love.
Such little things had filled your mind in Argos,
busied with this and that.
Once free of Sparta and in Troy where gold,
you thought, flowed like a river, you would spend
and spend, until your spendthrift hand
had drowned the town.
Your luxuries, your insolent excesses,
Menelaus' halls had grown too small for them.
Enough of that. By force you say he took you?
You cried out? Where? No one in Sparta heard you.

Young Castor was there and his brother too,
not yet among the stars.
And when you came to Troy and on your track the
        Greeks,
and death and agony in battle,
if they would tell you, "Greece has won today,"
you would praise this man here, Menelaus,
to vex my son, who feared him as a rival.
Then Troy had victories, and Menelaus
was nothing to you.
Looking to the successful side—oh yes,
you always followed there.
There was no right or wrong side in your eyes.
And now you talk of ropes—letting your body down
in secret from the wall, longing to go.
Who found you so?
Was there a noose around your neck?
A sharp knife in your hand? Such ways
as any honest woman would have found,
who loved the husband she had lost?
Often and often I would tell you, Go,
my daughter. My sons will find them other wives.
I will help you. I will send you past the lines
to the Greek ships. Oh, end this war
between our foes and us. But this was bitter to you.
In Paris' house you had your insolent way.
You liked to see the Eastern men fall at your feet.
These were great things to you.
Look at the dress you wear, your ornaments.
Is that the way to meet your husband?
You should not dare to breathe the same air with
        him.

Oh, men should spit upon you.
Humbly, in rags, trembling and shivering,
with shaven head—so you should come,
with shame at last, instead of shamelessness,
for all the wickedness you did.
King, one word more and I am done.
Give Greece a crown, be worthy of yourself.
Kill her. So shall the law stand for all women,
that she who plays false to her husband's bed,
shall die.

A WOMAN

O son of an ancient house, O King, now show
that you are worthy of your fathers.
The Greeks called you a woman, shamed you
with that reproach. Be strong. Be noble. Punish her.

MENELAUS (*impatiently.*)

I see it all as you do. We agree.
She left my house because she wanted to—
went to a stranger's bed. Her talk of Aphrodite—
big words, no more. (*Turns to* HELEN.) Go. Death
    is near.
Men there are waiting for you. In their hands are
    stones.
Die—a small price for the Greeks' long suffering.
You shall not any more dishonor me.

HELEN (*kneeling and clinging to him.*)

No! No! Upon my knees—see, I am praying to you.
It was the gods, not me. Oh, do not kill me.
Forgive.

HECUBA

The men she murdered. Think of those

who fought beside you—of their children too.
Never betray them. Hear that prayer.

MENELAUS (*roughly*.)

Enough, old woman. She is nothing to me.
Men, take her to the ships and keep her safe
until she sails.

HECUBA

But not with you! She must not set foot on your
    ship.

MENELAUS (*bitterly*.)

And why? Her weight too heavy for it?

HECUBA

A lover once, a lover always.

MENELAUS

(*pauses a moment to think*.)

Not so when what he loved has gone.
But it shall be as you would have it.
Not on the same ship with me. The advice is good.
And when she gets to Argos she shall die
a death hard as her heart.
So in the end she will become a teacher,
teach women chastity—no easy thing,
but yet her utter ruin will strike terror
into their silly hearts,
even women worse than she.

CHORUS

And so your temple in Ilium,
your altar of frankincense,
are given to the Greek,

the flame from the honey, the corn and the oil,
the smoke from the myrrh floating upward,
the holy citadel.
And Ida, the mountàin where the ivy grows,
and rivers from the snows rush through the glens,
and the.boundary wall of the world
where the first sunlight falls,
the blessed home of the dawn.

The sacrifice is gone, and the glad call
of dancers, and the prayers at evening to the gods
that last the whole night long.
Gone too the golden images,
and the twelve Moons, to Trojans holy.
Do you care, do you care, do you heed these things,
O God, from your throne in high heaven?
My city is perishing,
ending in fire and onrushing flame.

A WOMAN

O dear one, O my husband,
you are dead, and you wander
unburied, uncared for, while over-seas
the ships shall carry me,
swift-winged ships darting onward,
on to the land the riders love,
Argos, where the towers of stone
built by giants reach the sky.

ANOTHER

Children, our children.
At the gate they are crying, crying,
calling to us with tears,

Mother, I am all alone.
They are driving me away
to a black ship, and I cannot see you.

ANOTHER

Where, oh where? To holy Salamis,
with swift oars dipping?
Or to the crest of Corinth,
the city of two seas,
where the gates King Pelops built
for his dwelling stand?

ANOTHER

Oh, if only, far out to sea,
the crashing thunder of God
would fall down, down on Menelaus' ship,
crashing down upon her oars,
the Aegean's wild-fire light.
He it was drove me from Troy.
He is driving me in tears
over to Greece to slavery.

ANOTHER

And Helen, too, with her mirrors of gold,
looking and wondering at herself,
as pleased as a girl.
May she never come to the land of her fathers,
never see the hearth of her home,
her city, the temple with brazen doors
of goddess Athena.
Oh, evil marriage that brought
shame to Greece, the great,
and to the waters of Simois

sorrow and suffering.

(TALTHYBIUS *approaches with a few soldiers. He is carrying the dead child.*)

ANOTHER WOMAN

Before new sufferings are grown old
come other new.
Look, unhappy wives of Troy,
the dead Astyanax.
They threw him from the tower as one might pitch
    a ball.
Oh, bitter killing.
And now they have him there.

TALTHYBIUS

(*he gives the body into* HECUBA'S *arms.*)
One ship is waiting, Hecuba, to take aboard
the last of all the spoil Achilles' son was given,
and bear it with the measured beat of oars
to Thessaly's high headlands.
The chief himself has sailed because of news
he heard, his father's father
driven from his land by his own son.
So, more for haste even than before,
he went and with him went Andromache.
She drew tears from me there upon the ship
mourning her country, speaking to Hector's grave,
begging a burial for her child, your Hector's son,
who thrown down from the tower lost his life.
And this bronze-fronted shield, the dread of many
    a Greek,
which Hector used in battle,
that it should never, so she prayed,

hang in strange halls, her grief before her eyes,
nor in that bridal chamber where she must be a wife,
Andromache, this dead boy's mother.
She begged that he might lie upon it in his grave,
instead of cedar wood or vault of stone.
And in your arms she told me I must lay him,
for you to cover the body, if you still
have anything, a cloak left—
And to put flowers on him if you could,
since she has gone. Her master's haste
kept her from burying her child.
So now, whenever you have laid him out,
we'll heap the earth above him, then
up with the sails!
Do all as quickly as you can. One trouble
I saved you. When we passed Scamander's stream
I let the water run on him and washed his wounds.
I am off to dig his grave now, break up the hard
    earth.
Working together, you and I,
will hurry to the goal, oars swift for home.

HECUBA

Set the shield down—the great round shield of
    Hector.
I wish I need not look at it.
    (TALTHYBIUS *goes out with the soldiers.*)
You Greeks, your spears are sharp but not your
    wits.
You feared a child. You murdered him.
Strange murder. You were frightened, then? You
    thought

he might build up our ruined Troy? And yet
when Hector fought and thousands at his side,
we fell beneath you. Now, when all is lost,
the city captured and the Trojans dead,
a little child like this made you afraid.
The fear that comes when reason goes away—
Myself, I do not wish to share it.
   (*She dismisses the Greeks and their ways.*)
Beloved, what a death has come to you.
If you had fallen fighting for the city,
if you had known strong youth and love
and godlike power, if we could think
you had known happiness—if there is
happiness anywhere—
But now—you saw and knew, but with your soul
you did not know, and what was in your house
you could not use.
Poor little one. How savagely our ancient walls,
Apollo's towers, have torn away the curls
your mother's fingers wound and where she pressed
her kisses—here where the broken bone grins white—
Oh no—I cannot—
Dear hands, the same dear shape your father's had,
how loosely now you fall. And dear proud lips
forever closed. False words you spoke to me
when you would jump into my bed, call me sweet
      names
and tell me, Grandmother, when you are dead,
I'll cut off a great lock of hair and lead my soldiers
      all
to ride out past your tomb.

Not you, but I, old, homeless, childless,
must lay you in your grave, so young,
so miserably dead.
Dear God. How you would run to greet me.
And I would nurse you in my arms, and oh,
so sweet to watch you sleep. All gone.
What could a poet carve upon your tomb?
"A child lies here whom the Greeks feared and
    slew."
Ah, Greece should boast of that.
Child, they have taken all that was your father's,
but one thing, for your burying, you shall have,
the bronze-barred shield.
It kept safe Hector's mighty arm, but now
it has lost its master.
The grip of his own hand has marked it—dear to me
    then—
His sweat has stained the rim. Often and often
in battle it rolled down from brows and beard
while Hector held the shield close.
Come, bring such covering for the pitiful dead body
as we still have. God has not left us much
to make a show with. Everything I have
I give you, child.
    O men, secure when once good fortune comes—
fools, fools. Fortune's ways—
here now, there now. She springs
away—back—and away, an idiot's dance.
No one is ever always fortunate.

   (*The women have come in with coverings and
   garlands.*)

A WOMAN

Here, for your hands, they bring you clothing for
    the dead,
got from the spoils of Troy.

HECUBA

(*shrouding the body and putting garlands beside it.*)
Oh, not because you conquered when the horses
    raced,
or with the bow outdid your comrades,
your father's mother lays these wreaths beside you,
and of all that was yours, gives you this covering.
A woman whom God hates has robbed you,
taken your life, when she had taken your treasure
and ruined all your house.

A WOMAN

Oh, my heart! As if you touched it—touched it.
Oh, this was once our prince, great in the city.

HECUBA

So on your wedding day I would have dressed you,
the highest princess of the East your bride.
Now on your body I must lay the raiment,
all that is left of the splendor that was Troy's.
And the dear shield of Hector, glorious in battle,
mother of ten thousand triumphs won,
it too shall have its wreath of honor,
undying it will lie beside the dead.
More honorable by far than all the armor
Odysseus won, the wicked and the wise.

A WOMAN

You, O child, our bitter sorrow,

earth will now receive.
Mourn, O Mother.

HECUBA

Mourn, indeed.

A WOMAN

Weeping for all the dead.

HECUBA

Bitter tears.

A WOMAN

Your sorrows that can never be forgotten.
(*The funeral rite is now begun,* HECUBA *symbolically healing the wounds.*)

HECUBA

I heal your wounds; with linen I bind them.
Ah, in words only, not in truth—
a poor physician.
But soon among the dead your father
will care for you.

A WOMAN

Beat, beat your head.
Lift your hands and let them fall,
moving in measure.

HECUBA

O Women. Dearest—

A WOMAN

Oh, speak to us. Your cry—what does it mean?

HECUBA

Only this the gods would have,

pain for me and pain for Troy,
those they hated bitterly.
Vain, vain, the bulls we slew.
And yet—had God not bowed us down,
not laid us low in dust,
none would have sung of us or told our wrongs
in stories men will listen to forever.
Go: lay our dead in his poor grave,
with these last gifts of death given to him.
I think those that are gone care little
how they are buried. It is we, the living,
our vanity.

(*Women lift the shield with the body on it and
carry it out.*)

A WOMAN

Poor mother—her high hopes were stayed on you
and they are broken.
They called you happy at your birth,
a good man's son.
Your death was miserable exceedingly.

ANOTHER

Oh, see, see—
On the crested height of Troy
fiery hands. They are flinging torches.
Can it be
some new evil?
Something still unknown?

TALTHYBIUS

(*stops as he enters and speaks off stage.*)
Captains, attention. You have been given charge
to burn this city. Do not let your torches sleep.

Hurry the fire on.
When once the town is level with the ground
then off for home and glad goodbye to Troy.
And you, you Women—I will arrange for you
as well, one speech for everything—
whenever a loud trumpet-call is sounded,
go to the Greek ships, to embark.
Old woman, I am sorriest for you,
follow. Odysseus' men are here to get you.
He drew you—you must leave here as his slave.

HECUBA

The end then. Well—the height of sorrow, I stand
    there.
Troy is burning—I am going.
But—hurry, old feet, if you can,
a little nearer—here, where I can see
my poor town, say goodbye to her.
You were so proud a city, in all the East
the proudest. Soon your name the whole world
    knew,
will be taken from you. They are burning you
and leading us away, their slaves.
O God— What makes me say that word?
The gods— I prayed, they never listened.
Quick, into the fire— Troy, I will die with you.
Death then—oh, beautiful.

TALTHYBIUS

Out of your head, poor thing, with all you've suf-
    fered.
Lead her away— Hold her, don't be too gentle.
She must be taken to Odysseus.

Give her into his hands. She is his—
  (*Shakes his head.*)
his prize.
  (*It grows darker.*)

A WOMAN

Ancient of days, our country's Lord,
Father, who made us,
You see your children's sufferings.
Have we deserved them?

ANOTHER

He sees—but Troy has perished, the great city.
No city now, never again.

ANOTHER

Oh, terrible!
The fire lights the whole town up.
The inside rooms are burning.
The citadel—it is all flame now.

ANOTHER

Troy is vanishing.
War first ruined her.
And what was left is rushing up in smoke,
the glorious houses fallen.
First the spear and then the fire.

HECUBA

(*she stands up and seems to be calling to someone far
away.*)
Children, hear, your mother is calling.

A WOMAN (*gently.*)

They are dead, those you are speaking to.

HECUBA

My knees are stiff, but I must kneel.
Now, strike the ground with both my hands—

A WOMAN

I too, I kneel upon the ground.
I call to mine down there.
Husband, poor husband.

HECUBA

They are driving us like cattle—taking us away.

A WOMAN

Pain, all pain.

ANOTHER

To a slave's house, from my country.

HECUBA

Priam, Priam, you are dead,
and not a friend to bury you.
The evil that has found me—
do you know?

A WOMAN

No. Death has darkened his eyes.
He was good and the wicked killed him.

HECUBA

O dwellings of the gods and O dear city,
the spear came first and now
only the red flame lives there.

A WOMAN

Fall and be forgotten. Earth is kind.

ANOTHER

The dust is rising, spreading out like a great wing
    of smoke.
I cannot see my house.

ANOTHER

The name has vanished from the land,
and we are gone, one here, one there.
And Troy is gone forever.
    (*A great crash is heard.*)

HECUBA

Did you hear? Did you know—

A WOMAN

The fall of Troy—

ANOTHER

Earthquake and flood and the city's end—

HECUBA

Trembling body—old weak limbs,
you must carry me on to the new day of slavery.
    (*A trumpet sounds.*)

A WOMAN

Farewell, dear city.
Farewell, my country, where once my children lived.
On to the ships—
There below, the Greek ships wait.
    (*The trumpet sounds again and the women pass
    out.*)

V

A GREEK PSYCHOLOGICAL DRAMA

THE *PROMETHEUS* is unlike any other ancient play. Only in the most modern theater is a parallel to be found. There is no action in it. Aristotle, first of critics, said that drama depends on action, not character. There is only character in the *Prometheus*. The protagonist is motionless, chained to a rock. None of the other personages do anything. The drama consists solely in the unfolding of Prometheus' character by means of conversation. It is the exemplar that tragedy is essentially the suffering of a great soul who suffers greatly.

The dialogue is sustained with an admirable art. Each of the minor personages, however brief his appearance, is an individual, clearly characterized. Nothing in the picture is blurred. Force is a rough careless villain; Hephestus, the fire-god, a feeble,

kindly tool; the chorus, gentle conventional-minded
girls, who can find courage enough in a crisis; Hermes, a crude youth, much set up by his high office,
but beneath his grand assumption unsure of himself.

Ocean's character merits a fuller consideration
for the reason that the traditional view is that Attic
tragedy did not admit of comedy or humor. The
text books all tell us that it was unrelieved by any
lighter touch, and so gained an intensity of tragic
effect impossible to Shakespeare's checkered stage
of light and shade. But most readers will agree that
the comedy of Ocean's talk with Prometheus is beyond dispute. Ocean is a humorous creation, an
amiable, self-important old busybody, really dis-
tressed at Prometheus' hard fate, but bent upon
reading him a good lecture now that he has him
where he cannot run away; delighted to find himself the person of importance who has pull with
Zeus and can get that unpractical fool, Prometheus,
out of his not entirely undeserved punishment; but
underneath this superior attitude very uneasy because of Zeus, who "isn't so far off but he might
hear," and completely happy when Prometheus finally gives him a chance to save his face and run off
safely home. When this dialogue is understood as
humorous, the commentators and translators are re-
lieved of what has always been a stumbling block
to them, Ocean's four-footed bird. If it is accepted
as axiomatic that a Greek tragic drama cannot have
anything humorous in it, the bird with four feet undoubtedly presents difficulties. It is hard to see it
as a tragic adjunct. But the Athenian spectators were

at least as keen-witted as we are today, and when there appeared on the stage an enormous, grotesque bird with a pompous old man riding on its back, they had no more trouble than we should have in recognizing a comic interlude. Ocean is a figure of fun, and the steed he bestrides is there to give the audience the clue.

None of the points so far taken up will seem strange to the modern reader, but a real difficulty is presented by Io, a distracted, fleeing creature, quite mad, who seems now a girl and now a heifer, and by her talk with Prometheus, running into hundreds of lines, which consists largely of geography. These are matters that an ancient and a modern spectator would necessarily look at differently because so much of what was known to them is strange to us and vice versa. Io and her descendants were dear, familiar figures to Aeschylus' audience, always recognized with pleasure. On the other hand, Io's journey over the earth, which only the most devoted lover of Aeschylus today can help finding long, was delightful to the Greeks of long ago. The world outside of Greece was a place of wonder and mystery, and to lift the veil ever so little was to command the deepest interest. Geography was thrilling. It stayed so for a long time, as we know from one who won a lady's heart by stories of the Anthropophagi and men whose heads do grow beneath their shoulders. "These things to hear would Desdemona seriously incline." Shakespeare's audience and Aeschylus' were one on this point.

Milton's Satan is often called Prometheus injected with Christian theology, but the comparison falls to the ground. For all Satan's magnificence, he is, to use Prometheus' words, "young—young." Shame before the other spirits keeps him from submission quite as much as his own ambition. Beside him Prometheus seems experienced. He has learned what is important to him and what is not. He is calmly strong, loftily indifferent, never to be shaken, because he is sure, both of what he wants and what he means to do. He stands forever as the type of the great rebel.

A more interesting parallel is with Job, who when wronged to the utmost submits to irresistible power. He knows that all Jehovah has done to him is utter injustice, but in the end, confronted with the Almighty who can divide the waters and find the way of the thunder and set bounds to the sea, Job gives up: "I know that thou canst do all things. . . . Wherefore I abhor myself and repent in dust and ashes." Prometheus, too, is faced by irresistible force. His body is helplessly imprisoned, but his spirit is free. Just as with Job, the unconditional surrender is demanded of him. He refuses, and with his last words as the crumbling universe falls upon him, he asserts the injustice of the Almighty: "Behold me. I am wronged."

VI

THE *PROMETHEUS BOUND*
of AESCHYLUS

ꙏꙎꙏꙎꙏꙎꙏꙎꙏꙎꙏꙎꙏꙎꙏꙎꙏꙎꙏꙎꙏꙎꙏꙎꙏꙎꙏꙎꙏꙎꙏꙎꙏꙎ

(PROMETHEUS *by tradition was fastened to a peak
of the Caucasus.*)

FORCE

Far have we come to this far spot of earth,
this narrow Scythian land, a desert all untrodden.
God of the forge and fire, yours the task
the Father laid upon you.
To this high-piercing, head-long rock
in adamantine chains that none can break
bind him—him here, who dared all things.
Your flaming flower he stole to give to men,
fire, the master craftsman, through whose power
all things are wrought, and for such error now
he must repay the gods; be taught to yield
to Zeus' lordship and to cease
from his man-loving way.

HEPHESTUS

Force, Violence, what Zeus enjoined on you

has here an end. Your task is done.
But as for me, I am not bold to bind
a god, a kinsman, to this stormy crag.
Yet I must needs be bold.
His load is heavy who dares disobey the Father's
    word.
O high-souled child of Justice, the wise counselor,
against my will as against yours I nail you fast
in brazen fetters never to be loosed
to this rock peak, where no man ever comes,
where never voice or face of mortal you will see.
The shining splendor of the sun shall wither you.
Welcome to you will be the night
when with her mantle star-inwrought *
she hides the light of day.
And welcome then in turn the sun
to melt the frost the dawn has left behind.
Forever shall the intolerable present grind you
    down,
and he who will release you is not born.
Such fruit you reap for your man-loving way.
A god yourself, you did not dread God's anger,
but gave to mortals honor not their due,
and therefore you must guard this joyless rock—
no rest, no sleep, no moment's respite.
Groans shall your speech be, lamentation
your only words—all uselessly.
Zeus has no mind to pity. He is harsh,
like upstarts always.

---

* Shelley's adjective is the perfect translation. Anything else
would be less exact and less like Aeschylus.

FORCE

Well then, why this delay and foolish talk?
A god whom gods hate is abominable.

HEPHESTUS

The tie of blood has a strange power,
and old acquaintance too.

FORCE

And so say I—but don't you think
that disobedience to the Father's words
might have still stranger power?

HEPHESTUS

You're rough, as always. Pity is not in you.

FORCE

Much good is pity here. Why all this pother
that helps him not a whit?

HEPHESTUS

O skill of hand now hateful to me.

FORCE

Why blame your skill? These troubles here
were never caused by it. That's simple truth.

HEPHESTUS

Yet would it were another's and not mine.

FORCE

Trouble is everywhere except in heaven.
No one is free but Zeus.

HEPHESTUS

I know—I've not a word to say.

FORCE

Come then. Make haste. On with his fetters.
What if the Father sees you lingering?

HEPHESTUS

The chains are ready here if he should look.

FORCE

Seize his hands and master him.
Now to your hammer. Pin him to the rocks.

HEPHESTUS

All done, and quick work too.

FORCE

Still harder. Tighter. Never loose your hold.
For he is good at finding a way out where there is
        none.

HEPHESTUS

This arm at least he will not ever free.

FORCE

Buckle the other fast, and let him learn
with all his cunning he's a fool to Zeus.

HEPHESTUS

No one but he, poor wretch, can blame my work.

FORCE

Drive stoutly now your wedge straight through his
        breast,
the stubborn jaw of steel that cannot break.

HEPHESTUS

Alas, Prometheus, I grieve for your pain.

FORCE

You shirk your task and grieve for those Zeus hates?
Take care; you may need pity for yourself.

HEPHESTUS

You see a sight eyes should not look upon.

FORCE

I see one who has got what he deserves.
But come. The girdle now around his waist.

HEPHESTUS

What must be shall be done. No need to urge me.

FORCE

I will and louder too. Down with you now.
Make fast his legs in rings. Use all your strength.

HEPHESTUS

Done and small trouble.

FORCE

Now for his feet. Drive the nails through the flesh.
The judge is stern who passes on our work.

HEPHESTUS

Your tongue and face match well.

FORCE

Why, you poor weakling. Are you one to cast
a savage temper in another's face?

HEPHESTUS

Oh, let us go. Chains hold him, hand and foot.

FORCE

Run riot now, you there upon the rocks.

Go steal from gods to give their goods to men—
to men whose life is but a little day.
What will they do to lift these woes from you?
Forethought your name means, falsely named.
Forethought you lack and need now for yourself
if you would slip through fetters wrought like these.

(*Exeunt* FORCE, VIOLENCE, HEPHESTUS.)

PROMETHEUS

O air of heaven and swift-winged winds,
O running river waters,
O never numbered laughter of sea waves,
Earth, mother of all, Eye of the sun, all seeing,
on you I call.
Behold what I, a god, endure from gods.
See in what tortures I must struggle
through countless years of time.
This shame, these bonds, are put upon me
by the new ruler of the gods.
Sorrow enough in what is here and what is still to
    come.
It wrings groans from me.
When shall the end be, the appointed end?
And yet why ask?
All, all I knew before,
all that should be.
Nothing, no pang of pain
that I did not foresee.
Bear without struggle what must be.
Necessity is strong and ends our strife.
But silence is intolerable here.
So too is speech.

I am fast bound, I must endure.
I gave to mortals gifts.
I hunted out the secret source of fire.
I filled a reed therewith,
fire, the teacher of all arts to men,
the great way through.
These are the crimes that I must pay for,
pinned to a rock beneath the open sky.
But what is here? What comes?
What sound, what fragrance, brushed me with faint
     wings,
of deities or mortals or of both? *
Has someone found a way to this far peak
to view my agony? What else?
Look at me then, in chains, a god who failed,
the enemy of Zeus, whom all gods hate,
all that go in and out of Zeus' hall.
The reason is that I loved men too well.
Oh, birds are moving near me. The air murmurs
with swift and sweeping wings.
Whatever comes to me is terrible.

    (Enter CHORUS. *They are sea nymphs. It is clear
    from what follows that a winged car brings them
    on to the stage.*)

LEADER OF CHORUS

Oh, be not terrified, for friends are here,
each eager to be first,
on swift wings flying to your rock.
I prayed my father long
before he let me come.

* This line of Keats is the exact translation.

The rushing winds have sped me on.
A noise of ringing brass went through the sea-caves,
and for all a maiden's fears it drove me forth,
so swift, I did not put my sandals on,
but in my winged car I came to you.

PROMETHEUS

To see this sight—
Daughters of fertile Tethys,
children of Ocean who forever flows
unresting round earth's shores,
behold me, and my bonds
that bind me fast upon the rocky height
of this cleft mountain side,
keeping my watch of pain.

A SEA NYMPH

I look upon you and a mist of tears,
of grief and terror, rises as I see
your body withering upon the rocks,
in shameful fetters.
For a new helmsman steers Olympus.
By new laws Zeus is ruling without law.
He has put down the mighty ones of old.

PROMETHEUS

Oh, had I been sent deep, deep into earth,
to that black boundless place where go the dead,
though cruel chains should hold me fast forever,
I should be hid from sight of gods and men.
But now I am a plaything for the winds.
My enemies exult—and I endure.

ANOTHER NYMPH

What god so hard of heart to look on these things
    gladly?
Who, but Zeus only, would not suffer with you?
He is malignant always and his mind
unbending. All the sons of heaven
he drives beneath his yoke.
Nor will he make an end
until his heart is sated or until
someone, somehow, shall seize his sovereignty—
if that could be.

PROMETHEUS

And yet—and yet—all tortured though I am,
fast fettered here,
he shall have need of me, the lord of heaven,
to show to him the strange design
by which he shall be stripped of throne and scepter.
But he will never win me over
with honeyed spell of soft, persuading words,
nor will I ever cower beneath his threats
to tell him what he seeks.
First he must free me from this savage prison
and pay for all my pain.

ANOTHER

Oh, you are bold. In bitter agony
you will not yield.
These are such words as only free men speak.
Piercing terror stings my heart.
I fear because of what has come to you.
Where are you fated to put in to shore
and find a haven from this troubled sea?

Prayers cannot move,
persuasions cannot turn,
the heart of Kronos' son.

PROMETHEUS

I know that he is savage.
He keeps his righteousness at home.
But yet some time he shall be mild of mood,
when he is broken.
He will smooth his stubborn temper,
and run to meet me.
Then peace will come and love between us two.

LEADER

Reveal the whole to us. Tell us your tale.
What guilt does Zeus impute
to torture you in shame and bitterness?
Teach us, if you may speak.

PROMETHEUS

To speak is pain, but silence too is pain,
and everywhere is wretchedness.
When first the gods began to quarrel
and faction rose among them,
some wishing to throw Kronos out of heaven,
that Zeus, Zeus, mark you, should be lord,
others opposed, pressing the opposite,
that Zeus should never rule the gods,
then I, giving wise counsel to the Titans,
children of Earth and Heaven, could not prevail.
My way out was a shrewd one, they despised it,
and in their arrogant minds they thought to conquer
with ease, by their own strength.

But Justice, she who is my mother, told me—
Earth she is sometimes called,
whose form is one, whose name is many—
she told me, and not once alone,
the future, how it should be brought to pass,
that neither violence nor strength of arm
but only subtle craft could win.
I made all clear to them.
They scorned to look my way.
The best then left me was to stand with Zeus
in all good will, my mother with me,
and, through my counsel, the black underworld
covered, and hides within its secret depths
Kronos the aged and his host.
Such good the ruler of the gods had from me,
and with such evil he has paid me back.
There is a sickness that infects all tyrants,
they cannot trust their friends.
But you have asked a question I would answer:
What is my crime that I am tortured for?
Zeus had no sooner seized his father's throne
than he was giving to each god a post
and ordering his kingdom,
but mortals in their misery
he took no thought for.
His wish was they should perish
and he would then beget another race.
And there were none to cross his will save I.
I dared it, I saved men.
Therefore I am bowed down in torment,
grievous to suffer, pitiful to see.
I pitied mortals,

I never thought to meet with this.
Ruthlessly punished here I am
an infamy to Zeus.

LEADER

Iron of heart or wrought from rock is he
who does not suffer in your misery.
Oh, that these eyes had never looked upon it.
I see it and my heart is wrung.

PROMETHEUS

A friend must feel I am a thing to pity.

LEADER

Did you perhaps go even further still?

PROMETHEUS

I made men cease to live with death in sight.

LEADER

What potion did you find to cure this sickness?

PROMETHEUS

Blind hopes I caused to dwell in them.

ANOTHER SEA NYMPH

Great good to men that gift.

PROMETHEUS

To it I added the good gift of fire.

ANOTHER

And now the creatures of a day
have flaming fire?

PROMETHEUS

Yes, and learn many crafts therefrom.

LEADER

For deeds like these Zeus holds you guilty,
and tortures you with never ease from pain?
Is no end to your anguish set before you?

PROMETHEUS

None other except when it pleases him.

LEADER

It pleases him? What hope there? You must see
you missed your mark. I tell you this with pain
to give you pain.
But let that pass. Seek your deliverance.

PROMETHEUS

Your feet are free.
Chains bind mine fast.
Advice is easy for the fortunate.
All that has come I knew full well.
Of my own will I shot the arrow that fell short,
of my own will.
Nothing do I deny.
I helped men and found trouble for myself.
I knew—and yet not all.
I did not think to waste away
hung high in air upon a lonely rock.
But now, I pray you, no more pity
for what I suffer here. Come, leave your car,
and learn the fate that steals upon me,
all, to the very end.
Hear me, oh, hear me. Share my pain. Remember,
trouble may wander far and wide
but it is always near.

LEADER

You cry to willing ears, Prometheus.
Lightly I leave my swiftly speeding car
and the pure ways of air where go the birds.
I stand upon this stony ground.
I ask to hear your troubles to the end.

(*Enter* OCEAN *riding on a four-footed bird. The*
CHORUS *draw back, and he does not see them.*)

OCEAN

Well, here at last, an end to a long journey.
I've made my way to you, Prometheus.
This bird of mine is swift of wing
but I can guide him by my will,
without a bridle.
Now you must know, I'm grieved at your misfor-
tunes.
Of course I must be, I'm your kinsman.
And that apart, there's no one I think more of.
And you'll find out the truth of what I'm saying.
It isn't in me to talk flattery.
Come: tell me just what must be done to help you,
and never say that you've a firmer friend
than you will find in me.

PROMETHEUS

Oho! What's here? You? Come to see my troubles?
How did you dare to leave your ocean river,
your rock caves hollowed by the sea,
and stand upon the iron mother earth?
Was it to see what has befallen me,
because you grieve with me?
Then see this sight: here is the friend of Zeus,

who helped to make him master.
This twisted body is his handiwork.

OCEAN

I see, Prometheus. I do wish
You'd take some good advice.
I know you're very clever,
but real self-knowledge—that you haven't got.
New fashions have come in with this new ruler.
Why can't you change your own to suit?
Don't talk like that—so rude and irritating.
Zeus isn't so far off but he might hear,
and what would happen then would make these trou-
    bles
seem child's play.
You're miserable. Then do control your temper
and find some remedy.
Of course you think you know all that I'm saying.
You certainly should know the harm
that blustering has brought you.
But you're not humbled yet. You won't give in.
You're looking for more trouble.
Just learn one thing from me:
Don't kick against the pricks.
You see he's savage—why not? He's a tyrant.
He doesn't have to hand in his accounts.
Well, now I'm going straight to try
if I can free you from this wretched business.
Do you keep still. No more of this rash talking.
Haven't you yet learned with all your wisdom
the mischief that a foolish tongue can make?

PROMETHEUS

Wisdom? The praise for that is yours alone,
who shared and dared with me and yet were able
to shun all blame.
But—let be now. Give not a thought more to me.
You never would persuade him.
He is not easy to win over.
Be cautious. Keep a sharp look out,
or on your way back you may come to harm.

OCEAN

You counsel others better than yourself,
to judge by what I hear and what I see.
But I won't let you turn me off.
I really want to serve you.
And I am proud, yes, proud to say
I know that Zeus will let you go
just as a favor done to me.

PROMETHEUS

I thank you for the good will you would show me.
But spare your pains. Your trouble would be wasted.
The effort, if indeed you wish to make it,
could never help me.
Now you are out of harm's way. Stay there.
Because I am unfortunate myself
I would not wish that others too should be.
Not so. Even here the lot of Atlas, of my brother,
weighs on me. In the western country
he stands, and on his shoulders is the pillar
that holds apart the earth and sky,
a load not easy to be borne.

Pity too filled my heart when once I saw
swift Typhon overpowered.
Child of the Earth was he, who lived
in caves in the Cilician land,
a flaming monster with a hundred heads,
who rose up against all the gods.
Death whistled from his fearful jaws.
His eyes flashed glaring fire.
I thought he would have wrecked God's sov-
     ereignty.
But to him came the sleepless bolt of Zeus,
down from the sky, thunder with breath of flame,
and all his high boasts were struck dumb.
Into his very heart the fire burned.
His strength was turned to ashes.
And now he lies a useless thing,
a sprawling body, near the narrow sea-way
by Aetna, underneath the mountain's roots.
High on the peak the god of fire sits,
welding the molten iron in his forge,
whence sometimes there will burst
rivers red hot, consuming with fierce jaws
the level fields of Sicily,
lovely with fruits.
And that is Typhon's anger boiling up,
his darts of flame none may abide,
of fire-breathing spray,
scorched to a cinder though he is
by Zeus' bolt.
But you are no man's fool; you have no need
to learn from me. Keep yourself safe,

as you well know the way.
And I will drain my cup to the last drop,
until Zeus shall abate his insolence of rage.

OCEAN

And yet you know the saying,
when anger reaches fever heat
wise words are a physician.

PROMETHEUS

Not when the heart is full to bursting.
Wait for the crisis; then the balm will soothe.

OCEAN

But if one were discreet as well as daring—?
You don't see danger then? Advise me.

PROMETHEUS

I see your trouble wasted,
and you good-natured to the point of folly.

OCEAN

That's a complaint I don't mind catching.
Let be: I'll choose to seem a fool
if I can be a loyal friend.

PROMETHEUS

But he will lay to me all that you do.

OCEAN

There you have said what needs must send me home.

PROMETHEUS

Just so. All your lamenting over me
will not have got you then an enemy.

OCEAN

Meaning—the new possessor of the throne?

PROMETHEUS

Be on your guard. See that you do not vex him.

OCEAN

Your case, Prometheus, may well teach me—

PROMETHEUS

Off with you. Go—and keep your present mind.

OCEAN

You urge one who is eager to be gone.
For my four-footed bird is restless
to skim with wings the level ways of air.
He'll be well pleased to rest in his home stable.
(*Exit* OCEAN. *The* CHORUS *now come forward.*)

CHORUS

I mourn for you, Prometheus.
Desolation is upon you.
My face is wet with weeping.
Tears fall as waters which run continually.
The floods overflow me.
Terrible are the deeds of Zeus.
He rules by laws that are his own.
High is his spear above the others,
turned against the gods of old.
All the land now groans aloud,
mourning for the honor of the heroes of your race.
Stately were they, honored ever in the days of long
    ago.
Holy Asia is hard by.
Those that dwell there suffer in your trouble, great
    and sore.
In the Colchian land maidens live,

fearless in fight.
Scythia has a battle throng,
the farthest place of earth is theirs,
where marsh grass grows around Maeotis lake.
Arabia's flower is a warrior host;
high on a cliff their fortress stands,
Caucasus towers near;
men fierce as the fire, like the roar of the fire
they shout when the sharp spears clash.
All suffer with you in your trouble, great and sore.
Another Titan too, Earth mourns,
bound in shame and iron bonds.
I saw him, Atlas the god.
He bears on his back forever
the cruel strength of the crushing world
and the vault of the sky.
He groans beneath them.
The foaming sea-surge roars in answer,
the deep laments,
the black place of death far down in earth is moved
    exceedingly,
and the pure-flowing river waters grieve for him in
    his piteous pain.

PROMETHEUS

Neither in insolence nor yet in stubbornness
have I kept silence.
It is thought that eats my heart,
seeing myself thus outraged.
Who else but I, but I myself,
gave these new gods their honors?

Enough of that. I speak to you who know.
Hear rather all that mortals suffered.
Once they were fools. I gave them power to think.
Through me they won their minds.
I have no blame for them. All I would tell you
is my good will and my good gifts to them.
Seeing they did not see, nor hearing hear.
Like dreams they led a random life.
They had no houses built to face the sun,
of bricks or well-wrought wood,
but like the tiny ant who has her home
in sunless crannies deep down in the earth,
they lived in caverns.
The signs that speak of winter's coming,
of flower-faced spring, of summer's heat
with mellowing fruits,
were all unknown to them.
From me they learned the stars that tell the seasons,
their risings and their settings hard to mark.
And number, that most excellent device,
I taught to them, and letters joined in words.
I gave to them the mother of all arts,
hard working memory.
I, too, first brought beneath the yoke
great beasts to serve the plow,
to toil in mortals' stead.
Up to the chariot I led the horse that loves the rein,
the glory of the rich man in his pride.
None else but I first found
the seaman's car, sail-winged, sea-driven.
Such ways to help I showed them, I who have
no wisdom now to help myself.

LEADER

You suffer shame as a physician must
who cannot heal himself.
You who cured others now are all astray,
distraught of mind and faint of heart,
and find no medicine to soothe your sickness.

PROMETHEUS

Listen, and you shall find more cause for wonder.
Best of all gifts I gave them was the gift of healing.
For if one fell into a malady
there was no drug to cure, no draught, or soothing
    ointment.
For want of these men wasted to a shadow
until I showed them how to use
the kindly herbs that keep from us disease.
The ways of divination I marked out for them,
and they are many; how to know
the waking vision from the idle dream;
to read the sounds hard to discern;
the signs met on the road; the flight of birds,
eagles and vultures,
those that bring good or ill luck in their kind,
their way of life, their loves and hates
and council meetings.
And of those inward parts that tell the future,
the smoothness and the color and fair shape
that please the gods.
And how to wrap the flesh in fat
and the long thigh bone, for the altar fire
in honor to the gods.
So did I lead them on to knowledge

of the dark and riddling art.
The fire omens, too, were dim to them
until I made them see.
Deep within the earth are hidden
precious things for men,
brass and iron, gold and silver.
Would any say he brought these forth to light
until I showed the way?
No one, except to make an idle boast.
All arts, all goods, have come to men from me.

LEADER

Do not care now for mortals
but take thought for yourself, O evil-fated.
I have good hope that still loosed from your bonds
you shall be strong as Zeus.

PROMETHEUS

Not thus—not yet—is fate's appointed end,
fate that brings all to pass.
I must be bowed by age-long pain and grief.
So only will my bonds be loosed.
All skill, all cunning, is as foolishness
before necessity.

A SEA NYMPH

Who is the helmsman of necessity?

PROMETHEUS

Fate, threefold, Retribution, unforgetting.

ANOTHER

And Zeus is not so strong?

PROMETHEUS

He cannot shun what is foredoomed.

ANOTHER

And is he not foredoomed to rule forever?

PROMETHEUS

No word of that. Ask me no further.

ANOTHER

Some solemn secret hides behind your silence.

PROMETHEUS

Think of another theme. It is not yet
the time to speak of this.
It must be wrapped in darkness, so alone
I shall some time be saved
from shame and grief and bondage.

CHORUS

Zeus orders all things.
May he never set his might against purpose of mine,
like a wrestler in the match.
May I ever be found where feast the holy gods,
and the oxen are slain,
where ceaselessly flows the pathway
of Ocean, my father.
May the words of my lips forever
be free from sin.
May this abide with me and not depart
like melting snow.
Long life is sweet when there is hope
and hope is confident.
And it is sweet when glad thoughts make the heart
    grow strong,
and there is joy.
But you, crushed by a thousand griefs,

I look upon you and I shudder.
You did not tremble before Zeus.
You gave your worship where you would, to men,
a gift too great for mortals,
a thankless favor.
What help for you there? What defense in those
whose life is but from morning unto evening?
Have you not seen?
Their little strength is feebleness,
fast bound in darkness,
like a dream.
The will of man shall never break
the harmony of God.
This I have learned beholding your destruction.
Once I spoke different words to you
from those now on my lips.
A song flew to me.
I stood beside your bridal bed,
I sang the wedding hymn,
glad in your marriage.
And with fair gifts persuading her,
you led to share your couch
Hesione, child of the sea.

   (*Enter* io.)

                    IO

What land—what creatures here?
This, that I see—
A form storm-beaten,
bound to the rock.
Did you do wrong?
Is this your punishment?

You perish here.
Where am I?
Speak to a wretched wanderer.
Oh! Oh! he stings again—
the gadfly—oh, miserable!
But you must know he's not a gadfly.
He's Argus, son of Earth, the herdsman.
He has a thousand eyes.
I see him. Off! Keep him away!
No, he comes on.
His eyes can see all ways at once.
He's dead but no grave holds him.
He comes straight up from hell.
He is the huntsman,
and I his wretched quarry.
He drives me all along the long sea strand.
I may not stop for food or drink.
He has a shepherd's pipe,
a reed with beeswax joined.
Its sound is like the locust's shrilling,
a drowsy note—that will not let me sleep.
Oh, misery. Oh, misery.
Where is it leading me,
my wandering—far wandering.
What ever did I do,
how ever did I sin,
that you have yoked me to calamity,
O son of Kronos,
that you madden a wretched woman
driven mad by the gadfly of fear.
Oh, burn me in fire or hide me in earth
or fling me as food to the beasts of the sea.

Master, grant me my prayer.
Enough—I have been tried enough—
my wandering—long wandering.
Yet I have found no place
to leave my misery.
—I am a girl who speak to you,
but horns are on my head.

PROMETHEUS

Like one caught in an eddy, whirling round and
        round,
the gadfly drives you.
I know you, girl. You are Inachus' daughter.
You made the god's heart hot with love,
and Hera hates you. She it is
who drives you on this flight that never stops.

IO

How is it that you speak my father's name?
Who are you? Tell me for my misery.
Who are you, sufferer, that speak the truth
to one who suffers?
You know the sickness God has put upon me,
that stings and maddens me and drives me on
and wastes my life away.
I am a beast, a starving beast,
that frenzied runs with clumsy leaps and bounds,
oh, shame,
mastered by Hera's malice.
Who among the wretched
suffer as I do?
Give me a sign, you there.
Tell to me clearly

the pain still before me.
Is help to be found?
A medicine to cure me?
Speak, if you know.

PROMETHEUS

I will and in plain words,
as friend should talk to friend.
—You see Prometheus, who gave mortals fire.

IO

You, he who succored the whole race of men?
You, that Prometheus, the daring, the enduring?
Why do you suffer here?

PROMETHEUS

Just now I told the tale—

IO

But will you not still give to me a boon?

PROMETHEUS

Ask what you will. I know all you would learn.

IO

Then tell me who has bound you to this rock.

PROMETHEUS

Zeus was the mind that planned.
The hand that did the deed the god of fire.

IO

What was the wrong that you are punished for?

PROMETHEUS

No more. Enough of me.

IO

But you will tell the term set to my wandering?
My misery is great. When shall it end?

PROMETHEUS

Here not to know is best.

IO

I ask you not to hide what I must suffer.

PROMETHEUS

I do so in no grudging spirit.

IO

Why then delay to tell me all?

PROMETHEUS

Not through ill will. I would not terrify you.

IO

Spare me not more than I would spare myself.

PROMETHEUS

If you constrain me I must speak. Hear then—

LEADER

Not yet. Yield to my pleasure too.
For I would hear from her own lips
what is the deadly fate, the sickness
that is upon her. Let her say—then teach her
the trials still to come.

PROMETHEUS

If you would please these maidens, Io—
they are your father's sisters,
and when the heart is sorrowful, to speak

to those who will let fall a tear
is time well spent.

10

I do not know how to distrust you.
You shall hear all. And yet—
I am ashamed to speak,
to tell of that god-driven storm
that struck me, changed me, ruined me.
How shall I tell you who it was?
How ever to my maiden chamber
visions came by night,
persuading me with gentle words:
"Oh happy, happy girl,
Why are you all too long a maid
when you might marry with the highest?
The arrow of desire has pierced Zeus.
For you he is on fire.
With you it is his will to capture love.
Would you, child, fly from Zeus' bed?
Go forth to Lerna, to the meadows deep in grass.
There is a sheep-fold there,
an ox-stall, too, that holds your father's oxen—
so shall Zeus find release from his desire."
Always, each night, such dreams possessed me.
I was unhappy and at last I dared
to tell my father of these visions.
He sent to Pytho and far Dodona
man after man to ask the oracle
what he must say or do to please the gods.
But all brought answers back of shifting meaning,

hard to discern, like golden coins unmarked.
At last a clear word came. It fell upon him
like lightning from the sky. It told him
to thrust me from his house and from his country,
to wander to the farthest bounds of earth
like some poor dumb beast set apart
for sacrifice, whom no man will restrain.
And if my father would not, Zeus would send
his thunder-bolt with eyes of flame to end
his race, all, everyone.
He could not but obey such words
from the dark oracle. He drove me out.
He shut his doors to me—against his will
as against mine. Zeus had him bridled.
He drove him as he would.
Straightway I was distorted, mind and body.
A beast—with horns—look at me—
stung by a fly, who madly leaps and bounds.
And so I ran and found myself beside
the waters, sweet to drink, of Kerchneia
and Lerna's well-spring.
Beside me went the herdsman Argus,
the violent of heart, the earth-born,
watching my footsteps with his hundred eyes.
But death came to him, swift and unforeseen.
Plagued by a gadfly then, the scourge of God,
I am driven on from land to land.
So for what has been. But what still remains
of anguish for me, tell me.
Do not in pity soothe me with false tales.
Words strung together by a lie
are like a foul disease.

LEADER

Oh, shame. Oh, tale of shame.
Never, oh never, would I have believed that my ears
would hear words such as these, of strange meaning.
Evil to see and evil to hear,
misery, defilement, and terror.
They pierce my heart with a two-edged sword.
A fate like that—
I shudder to look upon Io.

PROMETHEUS

You are too ready with your tears and fears.
Wait for the end.

LEADER

Speak. Tell us, for when one lies sick,
to face with clear eyes all the pain to come
is sweet.

PROMETHEUS

What first you asked was granted easily,
to hear from her own lips her trials.
But for the rest, learn now the sufferings
she still must suffer, this young creature,
at Hera's hands. Child of Inachus,
keep in your heart my words, so you shall know
where the road ends. First to the sunrise,
over furrows never plowed, where wandering
    Scythians
live in huts of wattles made, raised high
on wheels smooth-rolling. Bows they have,
and they shoot far. Turn from them.

Keep to the shore washed by the moaning sea.
Off to the left live the Chalybians,
workers of iron. There be on your guard.
A rough people they, who like not strangers.
Here rolls a river called the Insolent,
true to its name. You cannot find a ford
until you reach the Caucasus itself,
highest of mountains. From beneath its brow
the mighty river rushes. You must cross
the summit, neighbor to the stars.
Then by the southward road, until you reach
the warring Amazons, men-haters, who one day
will found a city by the Thermodon,
where Salmydessus thrusts
a fierce jaw out into the sea that sailors hate,
stepmother of ships.
And they will bring you on your way right gladly
to the Cimmerian isthmus, by a shallow lake,
Maeotis, at the narrows.
Here you must cross with courage.
And men shall tell forever of your passing.
The strait shall be named for you, Bosporus,
Ford of the Cow. There leave the plains of Europe,
and enter Asia, the great Continent.
—Now does he seem to you, this ruler of the gods,
evil, to all, in all things?
A god desired a mortal—drove her forth
to wander thus.
A bitter lover you have found, O girl,
for all that I have told you is not yet
the prelude even.

IO

Oh, wretched, wretched.

PROMETHEUS

You cry aloud for this? What then
when you have learned the rest?

LEADER

You will not tell her of more trouble?

PROMETHEUS

A storm-swept sea of grief and ruin.

IO

What gain to me is life? Oh, now to fling myself
down from this rock peak to the earth below,
and find release there from my trouble.
Better to die once than to suffer
through all the days of life.

PROMETHEUS

Hardly would you endure my trial,
whose fate it is not ever to find death
that ends all pain. For me there is no end
until Zeus falls from power.

IO

Zeus fall from power?

PROMETHEUS

You would rejoice, I think, to see that happen?

IO

How could I not, who suffer at his hands?

PROMETHEUS

Know then that it shall surely be.

IO

But who will strip the tyrant of his scepter?

PROMETHEUS

He will himself and his own empty mind.

IO

How? Tell me, if it is not wrong to ask.

PROMETHEUS

He will make a marriage that will vex him.

IO

Goddess or mortal, if it may be spoken?

PROMETHEUS

It may not be. Seek not to know.

IO

His wife shall drive him from his throne?

PROMETHEUS

Her child shall be more than his father's match.

IO

And is there no way of escape for him?

PROMETHEUS

No way indeed, unless my bonds are loosed.

IO

But who can loose them against Zeus' will?

PROMETHEUS

A son of yours—so fate decrees.

IO

What words are these? A child of mine shall free
you?

PROMETHEUS

Ten generations first must pass and then three more.

IO

Your prophecy grows dim through generations.

PROMETHEUS

So let it be. Seek not to know your trials.

IO

Do not hold out a boon and then withdraw it.

PROMETHEUS

One boon of two I will bestow upon you.

IO

And they are? Speak. Give me the choice.

PROMETHEUS

I give it you: the hardships still before you,
or his name who shall free me. Choose.

LEADER

Of these give one to her, but give to me
a grace as well—I am not quite unworthy.
Tell her where she must wander, and to me
tell who shall free you. It is my heart's desire.

PROMETHEUS

And to your eagerness I yield.
Hear, Io, first, of your far-driven journey.
And bear in mind my words, inscribe them
upon the tablets of your heart.
When you have crossed the stream that bounds
the continents, turn to the East where flame
the footsteps of the sun, and pass

along the sounding sea to Cisthene.
Here on the plain live Phorcys' children, three,
all maidens, very old, and shaped like swans,
who have one eye and one tooth to the three.
No ray of sun looks ever on that country,
nor ever moon by night. Here too their sisters dwell.
And they are three, the Gorgons, winged,
with hair of snakes, hateful to mortals.
Whom no man shall behold and draw again
the breath of life. They garrison that place.
And yet another evil sight, the hounds of Zeus,
who never bark, griffins with beaks like birds.
The one-eyed Arimaspi too, the riders,
who live beside a stream that flows with gold,
a way of wealth. From all these turn aside.
Far off there is a land where black men live,
close to the sources of the sun, whence springs
a sun-scorched river. When you reach it,
go with all care along the banks up to
the great descent, where from the mountains
the holy Nile pours forth its waters
pleasant to drink from. It will be your guide
to the Nile land, the Delta. A long exile
is fated for you and your children here.
If what I speak seems dark and hard to know,
ask me again and learn all clearly.
For I have time to spare and more
than I could wish.

LEADER
If in your story of her fatal journey
there is yet somewhat left to tell her,

speak now. If not, give then to us
the grace we asked. You will remember.

PROMETHEUS

The whole term of her roaming has been told.
But I will show she has not heard in vain,
and tell her what she suffered coming hither,
in proof my words are true.
A moving multitude of sorrows were there,
too many to recount, but at the end
you came to where the levels of Molossa
surround the lofty ridge of Dodona,
seat of God's oracle.
A wonder past belief is there, oak trees that speak.
They spoke, not darkly but in shining words,
calling you Zeus' glorious spouse.
The frenzy seized you then. You fled
along the sea-road washed by the great inlet,
named for God's mother. Up and down you wan-
    dered,
storm-tossed. And in the time to come that sea
shall have its name from you, Ionian,
that men shall not forget your journey.
This is my proof to you my mind can see
farther than meets the eye.
From here the tale I tell is for you all,
and of the future, leaving now the past.
There is a city, Canobus, at the land's end,
where the Nile empties, on new river soil.
There Zeus at last shall make you sane again,
stroking you with a hand you will not fear.
And from this touch alone you will conceive

and bear a son, a swarthy man,
whose harvest shall be reaped on many fields,
all that are washed by the wide-watered Nile.
In the fifth generation from him, fifty sisters
will fly from marriage with their near of kin,
who, hawks in close pursuit of doves, a-quiver
with passionate desire, shall find that death
waits for the hunters on the wedding night.
God will refuse to them the virgin bodies.
Argos will be the maidens' refuge, to their suitors
a slaughter dealt by women's hands,
bold in the watches of the night.
The wife shall kill her husband,
dipping her two-edged sword in blood.
O Cyprian goddess, thus may you come to my foes.
One girl, bound by love's spell, will change
her purpose, and she will not kill
the man she lay beside, but choose the name
of coward rather than be stained with blood.
In Argos she will bear a kingly child—
a story overlong if all were told.
Know this, that from that seed will spring
one glorious with the bow, bold-hearted,
and he shall set me free.
This is the oracle my mother told me,
Justice, who is of old, Earth's daughter.
But how and where would be too long a tale,
nor would you profit.

10

Oh, misery. Oh, misery.
A frenzy tears me.

Madness strikes my mind.
I burn. A frantic sting—
an arrow never forged with fire.
My heart is beating at its walls in terror.
My eyes are whirling wheels.
Away. Away. A raging wind of fury
sweeps through me.
My tongue has lost its power.
My words are like a turbid stream,
wild waves that dash against a surging sea,
the black sea of madness.

(*Exit* 10.)

CHORUS

Wise, wise was he,
who first weighed this in thought
and gave it utterance:
Marriage within one's own degree is best,
not with one whom wealth has spoiled,
nor yet with one made arrogant by birth.
Such as these he must not seek
who lives upon the labor of his hands.
Fate, dread deity,
may you never, oh, never behold me
sharing the bed of Zeus.
May none of the dwellers in heaven
draw near to me ever.
Terrors take hold of me
seeing her maidenhood
turning from love of man,
torn by Hera's hate,
driven in misery.

For me, I would not shun marriage nor fear it,
so it were with my equal.
But the love of the greater gods,
from whose eyes none can hide,
may that never be mine.
To war with a god-lover is not war,
it is despair.
For what could I do,
or where could I fly
from the cunning of Zeus?

PROMETHEUS

In very truth shall Zeus, for all his stubborn pride,
be humbled, such a marriage he will make
to cast him down from throne and power.
And he shall be no more remembered.
The curse his father put on him
shall be fulfilled.
The curse that he cursed him with as he fell
from his age-long throne.
The way from such trouble no one of the gods
can show him save I.
These things I know and how they shall come to
    pass.
So let him sit enthroned in confidence,
trust to his crashing thunder high in air,
shake in his hands his fire-breathing dart.
Surely these shall be no defense,
but he will fall, in shame unbearable.
Even now he makes ready against himself
one who shall wrestle with him and prevail,
a wonder of wonders, who will find

a flame that is swifter than lightning,
a crash to silence the thunder,
who will break into pieces the sea-god's spear,
the bane of the ocean that shakes the earth.
Before this evil Zeus shall be bowed down.
He will learn how far apart are a king and a slave.

LEADER

These words of menace on your tongue
speak surely only your desire.

PROMETHEUS

They speak that which shall surely be—
and also my desire.

LEADER

And we must look to see Zeus mastered?

PROMETHEUS

Yes, and beneath a yoke more cruel than this I bear.

LEADER

You have no fear to utter words like these?

PROMETHEUS

I am immortal—and I have no fear.

ANOTHER SEA NYMPH

But agony still worse he might inflict—

PROMETHEUS

So let him do. All that must come I know.

ANOTHER

The wise bow to the inescapable.

PROMETHEUS

Be wise then. Worship power.

Cringe before each who wields it.
To me Zeus counts as less than nothing.
Let him work his will, show forth his power
for his brief day, his little moment
of lording it in heaven.
—But see. There comes a courier from Zeus,
a lackey in his new lord's livery.
Some curious news is surely on his lips.

(*Enter* HERMES.)

HERMES

You trickster there, you biter bitten,
sinner against the gods, man-lover, thief of fire,
my message is to you.
The great father gives you here his orders:
Reveal this marriage that you boast of,
by which he shall be hurled from power.
And, mark you, not in riddles, each fact clearly.
—Don't make me take a double journey, Prometheus.
    You can see Zeus isn't going to be made kinder
    by this sort of thing.

PROMETHEUS

Big words and insolent. They well become you,
O lackey of the gods.
Young—young—your thrones just won,
you think you live in citadels grief cannot reach.
Two dynasties I have seen fall from heaven,
and I shall see the third fall fastest,
most shamefully of all.
Is it your thought to see me tremble
and crouch before your upstart gods?

Not so—not such a one am I.
Make your way back. You will not learn from me.

HERMES

Ah, so? Still stubborn? Yet this willfulness
has anchored you fast in these troubled waters.

PROMETHEUS

And yet I would not change my lot
with yours, O lackey.

HERMES

Better no doubt to be slave to a rock
than be the Father's trusted herald.

PROMETHEUS

I must be insolent when I must speak to insolence.

HERMES

You are proud, it seems, of what has come to you

PROMETHEUS

I proud? May such pride be
the portion of my foes.—I count you of them.

HERMES

You blame me also for your sufferings?

PROMETHEUS

In one word, all gods are my enemies.
They had good from me. They return me evil.

HERMES

I heard you were quite mad.

PROMETHEUS

Yes, I am mad, if to abhor such foes is madness.

HERMES

You would be insufferable, Prometheus, if you were
    not so wretched.

PROMETHEUS

Alas!

HERMES

Alas? That is a word Zeus does not understand.

PROMETHEUS

Time shall teach it him, gray time,
that teaches all things.

HERMES

It has not taught you wisdom yet.

PROMETHEUS

No, or I had not wrangled with a slave.

HERMES

It seems that you will tell the Father nothing.

PROMETHEUS

Paying the debt of kindness that I owe him?

HERMES

You mock at me as though I were a child.

PROMETHEUS

A child you are or what else has less sense
if you expect to learn from me.
There is no torture and no trick of skill,
there is no force, which can compel my speech,
until Zeus wills to loose these deadly bonds.
So let him hurl his blazing bolt,
and with the white wings of the snow,

with thunder and with earthquake,
confound the reeling world.
None of all this will bend my will
to tell him at whose hands he needs must fall.

HERMES

I urge you, pause and think if this will help you.

PROMETHEUS

I thought long since of all. I planned for all.

HERMES

Submit, you fool. Submit. In agony learn wisdom.

PROMETHEUS

Go and persuade the sea wave not to break.
You will persuade me no more easily.
I am no frightened woman, terrified
at Zeus' purpose. Do you think to see me
ape women's ways, stretch out my hands
to him I hate, and pray him for release?
A world apart am I from prayer for pity.

HERMES

Then all I say is said in vain.
Nothing will move you, no entreaty
soften your heart.
Like a young colt new-bridled,
you have the bit between your teeth,
and rear and fight against the rein.
But all this vehemence is feeble bombast.
A fool, bankrupt of all but obstinacy,
is the poorest thing on earth.
Oh, if you will not hear me, yet consider
the storm that threatens you from which

you cannot fly, a great third wave of evil.
Thunder and flame of lightning will rend
this jagged peak. You shall be buried deep,
held by a splintered rock.
After long length of time you will return
to see the light, but Zeus' winged hound,
an eagle red with blood,
shall come a guest unbidden to your banquet.
All day long he will tear to rags your body,
great rents within the flesh,
feasting in fury on the blackened liver.
Look for no ending to this agony
until a god will freely suffer for you,
will take on him your pain, and in your stead
descend to where the sun is turned to darkness,
the black depths of death.
Take thought: this is no empty boast
but utter truth. Zeus does not lie.
Each word shall be fulfilled.
Pause and consider. Never think
self-will is better than wise counsel.

LEADER

To us the words he speaks are not amiss.
He bids you let your self-will go and seek
good counsel. Yield.
For to the wise a failure is disgrace.

PROMETHEUS

These tidings that the fellow shouts at me
were known to me long since.
A foe to suffer at the hands of foes
is nothing shameful.

Then let the twisting flame of forked fire
be hurled upon me. Let the very air
be rent by thunder-crash.
Savage winds convulse the sky,
hurricanes shake the earth from its foundations,
the waves of the sea rise up and drown the stars,
and let me be swept down to hell,
caught in the cruel whirlpool of Necessity.
He cannot kill me.

HERMES

Why, these are ravings you may hear from madmen.
His case is clear. Frenzy can go no further.
You maids who pity him, depart, be swift.
The thunder peals and it is merciless.
Would you too be struck down?

LEADER

Speak other words, another counsel,
if you would win me to obey.
Now, in this place, to urge
that I should be a coward is intolerable.
I choose with him to suffer what must be.
Not to stand by a friend—there is no evil
I count more hateful.
I spit it from my mouth.

HERMES

Remember well I warned you,
when you are swept away in utter ruin.
Blame then yourselves, not fate, nor ever say
that Zeus delivered you
to a hurt you had not thought to see.

With open eyes,
not suddenly, not secretly,
into the net of utter ruin
whence there is no escape,
you fall by your own folly.

   (*Exit* HERMES.)

PROMETHEUS

An end to words. Deeds now.
The world is shaken.
The deep and secret way of thunder
is rent apart.
Fiery wreaths of lightning flash.
Whirlwinds toss the swirling dust.
The blasts of all the winds are battling in the air,
and sky and sea are one.
On me the tempest falls.
It does not make me tremble.
O holy Mother Earth, O air and sun,
behold me. I am wronged.

VII

AN APOLOGIA

ⴡⴡⴡⴡⴡⴡⴡⴡⴡⴡⴡⴡⴡⴡⴡⴡⴡⴡⴡⴡⴡⴡⴡⴡⴡⴡⴡⴡⴡⴡⴡⴡⴡⴡⴡⴡⴡ

A LARGE PART OF
a Greek tragedy consists of poems written in a way
that is completely foreign to English poetry and,
indeed, to the poetry of any other language of the
Western world. There is nothing like it even in
Latin poetry. In the *Agamemnon*, of the 1,673 lines
of the play, 900 are dialogue, the rest is made up of
these strange poems. They marked the division of
the play into scenes, as a curtain does with us. In
all probability they were not spoken but sung. The
performers, whom the Greeks called the chorus—
the primary meaning of the word in Greek means
dance—were not on the stage, but in front of it, and
they took, as a rule, little or no part in the action of
the play. Their lines, however, usually bore upon
the action and were often a kind of commentary
on what was happening. In contrast to the dialogue,
which was always written in a six-foot measure, felt
by the Greeks, according to Aristotle, to be "better

adapted for being spoken" than any other, the choral
poems were never written in a fixed measure, but
in most varying meters that changed constantly
within a single verse, often from line to line. We
have no parallel to this in our poetry and the sound
falls strangely on our ears. An English poem always
has the same rhythmic movement. It would offend
us to have a poem that began in the measure of

There is sweet music here that softer falls—

swing into that of

It was many and many a year ago—

The Greek found such changes natural and completely consonant with poetic melody:

Now is she mad of mood and by some God possessed.
Her words—wild they ring,
as for her fate she mourns. So wails
ever the bird with wings of brown, musical nightingale.

No—but a house God hates.
Murders and strangling deaths.
Kin—striking down kin. Oh, they kill men here.
House that knows evil and evil. The floor drips red.

On the printed page these lines have the look of free
verse. There is no regularity in the length of line
any more than in the accents, but the resemblance
to our own free verse ends there. Greatly as the
lines given above vary, each has its own strongly
marked rhythm. Here is no question of subtle ca-
dences which to many a reader give only the effect
of prose. They are unmistakably metrical. Further-
more, the Greek choruses are written in sets of

similar verses and the two that belong to the same
set must correspond in the most meticulous way.
The poet was free to do what he wanted with the
first verse. Every line might be in a different meter.
But the second verse had to follow the irregularity
of the first, line for line and syllable for syllable.
Each line had to have not only exactly the same
accents as the corresponding line in the companion
verse, but exactly the same number of syllables. The
comparison with free verse does not carry us very
far. In truth, as compared with the Greeks even our
most academic poets are careless metricians. Milton
writes:

> Thus with the year
> Seasons return, but not to me returns
> Day, or the sweet approach of Eve'n or Morn,
> Or sight of vernal bloom or summer's rose,
> Or flocks, or herds, or human face divine—

and we hear all the lines alike. We never notice that
the poet has begun the first two lines with an accented syllable and in the two following has changed
to an accent on the second syllable. We feel no
difficulty in reading them; they all sound exactly the
same to our ear. Not so the Greeks. If in two corresponding lines of a choral ode Aeschylus had done
what Milton did, it would have been wrong to his
hearers; it would have offended their ear. To each
age its own poetic license. Modern poets may vary
the number of syllables and the position of the initial
accent; the Greek was free to vary his rhythmic
measure.

There is nothing in the poetry we know to help

us to understand this usage. Greek choruses are written in a way that is outside of our experience. Anyone, therefore, who tries to reproduce the meters of the original has this great difficulty to meet, the fact of their strangeness to our ears. A translation has completely failed which fails to mediate between the writer and the reader. A translator who adopts a method of writing that will inevitably at the outset sound queer to the reader, must make his apologia.

There were two main reasons that led me to keep to the original meters in translating the choral odes. First of all was the consideration that a poet's choice of meter is a matter scarcely less personal or less important than his choice of a subject. One has only to fancy any poem transposed into the meter of another to perceive how essential a part of each is the measure it is written in:

O wild west wind, thou breath of autumn's being—

changed to the meter of

> One more unfortunate,
> Weary of breath—

or

> St. Agnes' Eve— Ah, bitter chill it was—

to

> Hear the music of the bells—silver bells—

The transposition is in fact impossible to conceive of. The meter the poet chose is essential to his poem. To me, who had been familiar with the sound of the choruses of the *Agamemnon* from my youth and knew much of them by heart, it seemed even more impossible to conceive of changing them into other meters than to do so to an English poem, and my feeling was based on fact. For meter was more important to the Greeks than it is to us; it played a bigger role with them. They felt it in a way we do not; they perceived a connection between the sense and the sound which we are not aware of. There was to their ear some actual correspondence. Emotions could be expressed by meters as well as by words; if a poem changed from grief to joy, from tranquillity to passion, it was to be expected that the meter would change too.

Aeschylus has Cassandra speak of her peaceful childhood in a grave, quiet measure:

> Scamander's stream,
> waters my fathers drank,
> once on your banks a girl,
> sorrow-doomed, was reared,
> tenderly cherished there.

Then she thinks of the terrible death so near her and the meter becomes swifter and more uneven:

> Now to the river loud of lamentation,
> the shores of pain, I go to prophesy.

The chorus answer her sadly and calmly:

> Your pain—bitter pain,
> thrills as a sorrowful song,
> breaking the heart to hear.

Helen's beauty is described in a smooth, flowing measure:

So once there came
to the town of Ilium
  what seemed
a very dream of peace,
the calm no wind stirs ever,
  a rich man's
fragile shining jewel,
soft eyes that glancing sped a dart,
flower of love that pierced men's hearts.

Then the thought of all the misery that beauty
caused arouses the poet to anger and the meter
changes to one that carries the very sound of words
passionately spoken:

But she swerved sharp and she worked out
to a bitter end her bridal.
In her house base, to her friends base,
and she brought doom where she entered.

It is true that the reasons for the changes in meter
are often not so clear as in the instances cited, and
are frequently quite unintelligible to us, but when
we can perceive them they illuminate the poetry
and give it an added meaning. They are more than
a curious illustration of the strange ways of poets
of long ago.

One more explanation is due the reader. The
scholars say that in the choruses the length of the
line is a matter of great importance, as it is of course
in our own rhyming poetry. It is superfluous, perhaps, to say that Greek poetry was not rhymed. But
in my translation it has often been impossible to
keep to the lines as arranged by any editor—no two
editors are in complete agreement on this point—

because frequently in the original, one accented syllable follows another in the same line. This did not trouble the Greeks for reasons that lie deep within the structure of the Greek language, but it would be an almost insuperable difficulty to the English reader. We almost never accent two successive syllables in a single line. Shelley's "O Wild West Wind" is one of the rare examples. But they are so rare, they are always hard to recognize.

In the lines,

> On a cloud I saw a child
> And he laughing said to me—

we know from the first line that in the second, *and*, not *he*, must be accented. We read it thus without trouble because we expect the line to have the same accents as the preceding. But write these two as one line and we should go astray:

On a cloud I saw a child and he laughing said to me—

We should infallibly, at first, accent not *and*—which follows an accented word—but *he*, and completely lose the rhythm. Therefore, to make the Greek accent intelligible to the reader, I have usually broken up lines in which this juxtaposition of accented words occurs, so that the second word shall begin a line. Just as in Blake's lines given above, whereby any difficulty for the reader is avoided, I write,

> But if once blood
> fall to the ground,
>   dark tide of death—

instead of the single line the scholars use. There is
no other way to make the meter comprehensible to
us. Also, it must be remembered, these choral odes
were poems not to be read, but to be heard, and to
the hearer it is a matter of complete indifference
whether words that are spoken—provided there is
no rhyme—are conceived of as making up one line
or more.

My reasons then for keeping to the meters of the
original were, first, to give the reader the sound of
these strange and—when one grows used to them—
beautiful measures, and secondly, to preserve the
connection between the rhythm and the sense,
which is their distinguishing feature. It has proved
an undertaking of extreme difficulty, involving as
it did the reproduction of each line syllable by
syllable. To have given merely a reproduction of
the general effect of the measures would have been
a comparatively easy task, but for the most part I
have reproduced accurately the Greek. Occasionally
I have allowed myself to use two short syllables instead of one long—a liberty, I may say, Aeschylus
occasionally allows himself—and also, very occasionally, to add an *a* or *the* to the beginning of a line,
but these are the only variations—at least, the only
intentional ones. No doubt, I have slipped up at
times. Still, putting altogether aside the fact of the
structural difference between Greek and English
poetry, due to the difference between the two lan-
guages, my verses read the way we read the Greek
verses today. They have the same number of syllables and the same accents.

It has seemed to me that with all the difficulty involved there was a certain gain from the point of view of the translation. I had for the most part to be as brief as the Greek, as bare as the Greek. I was saved in a measure from the translator's great temptation, to expand, to interpret and make clear when the original does not.

If, however, the reader is put off by the strangeness of the Greek way of writing this kind of poetry, then the experiment has been a failure. Indeed, to make a version of one of the greatest poems in the world, that is awkward or ugly or both, is to do something worse than fail. As I have said before, no writer can judge the effect of his work as little as a translator can. The Greek way of writing is so familiar to me and so beautiful, my approximation to its metrical measures seems to me better than a transposition into an English measure.

VIII

HEART WITH STRINGS OF STEEL

ᴌᴜᴜᴜᴜᴜᴜᴜᴜᴜᴜᴜᴜᴜᴜᴜᴜᴜᴜᴜᴜᴜᴜᴜᴜᴜᴜᴜᴜᴜᴜᴜᴜᴜ

Aᴇꜱᴄʜʏʟᴜꜱ ᴡᴀꜱ
the eldest of the three Greek tragic poets. He was the first writer of tragedy. Not the first, surely, to perceive it; where great souls suffer inexplicably, there tragedy is, never to be easily concealed or ignored. It has in it that which startles the mind to attention and brings the spirit up sharp against the enigma of human life. In all ages men must have discerned it and been baffled by it, but Aeschylus was the first to write it. He conceived it so grandly and expressed it so adequately that there have been only three others fit to stand beside him, and those three, Sophocles, Euripides and Shakespeare, did their work after him, after he had put tragedy into literature.

The *Agamemnon* holds the chief place among the seven plays of his which have come down to us.

The trilogy of which it is a part, was his last play; he was within two years of his death when he produced it. More than forty years before, he had brought out his first play, and during all that time his genius had gone on developing. It was at its height when he died.

The play belongs to Clytemnestra, his heroine. Her only rival is the chorus into whose mouth Aeschylus puts the greatest poetry he wrote. But Clytemnestra dominates the scene. Agamemnon, her husband, when he sailed for Troy ten years before, had sacrificed their daughter to the gods to get favorable winds for the fleet, and at that moment Clytemnestra made up her mind to kill him if ever he got back. The pathos and the horror of that sacrifice are vividly described; Aeschylus intends us to realize what the girl's mother must have felt.

> And all her prayers, cries of Father, Father,
> her maiden life—
> these they held as nothing.
> Upon the ground
> fell her robe of saffron,
> and from her eyes
> sped an arrow
> that pierced with pity those that slew her.
> I see her there, a picture clear before my eyes.
> She strives to speak, as oftentimes,
> her father near, at the banquet table,
> she used to sing, the little maid,
> pure voice raised,
> honoring her father loved—

There was reason for Clytemnestra's implacable hatred. We are never allowed to forget her anguish of grief for her daughter, as well as her abhorrence of the father who killed his child. She speaks to the chorus of "What those dead suffered—that pain which never sleeps." It had never slept for her during all the ten years. It made her plan coolly and ruthlessly to murder her husband at the very moment of his triumphant home-coming.

She receives him upon his return with words of exultant joy that he has come back safe. She is exultant. Under their seeming falseness the words are true. His death before Troy would never have satisfied her. Her hand must strike him down. When he finally enters the palace where she will kill him, she pauses for a moment on the steps and prays, with what intensity,

God, God, fulfillment is with thee. Fulfill my prayers. In thy care rests that which shall be fulfilled.

She is not a murderer in her own eyes; she is an executioner.

When the deed is done she comes out before the palace to proclaim it, but not defiantly. She is so justified to herself, she does not think of others. She has no idea of excusing herself until later the accusations of the chorus drive her to do so. She speaks with an overpowering rush of immense relief. Those ten years of desperate resolve are over.

Long years ago I planned. Now it is done.
Old hatred ended. It was slow in coming,
but it came—

She is magnificent as she stands there, unshaken, speaking out all that she did and all that she felt,

without a thought of concealment. His blood is on
her face and dress and she is glad.

> So there he lay, and as he gasped, his blood
> spouted and splashed me with dark spray—a dew
> of death, sweet to me as heaven's sweet rain drops
> when the corn-land buds.

As Homer told the story, she killed Agamemnon
because she had betrayed him with another man,
but in Aeschylus, even though she is the man's
mistress and loves him, she kills her husband because
he killed their daughter, for that reason only. When
the chorus turn upon her and she must justify herself, her answer to them is,

> He cared no more than if a beast should die,
> when flocks are plenty in the fleecy fold,
> and slew his daughter, dearest anguish borne
> by me in travail—slew her for a charm
> against the Thracian winds.

Into that vengeance her lover did not come at all.
She struck the blow, not he. The horrified chorus
ask her,

> Who will make his grave?
> You? Will you dare who dared to kill him?

She answers, Yes.

> The hands that he fell by and died by shall bury him.
> One—one will receive him in love where he goes,
>   fitly—his daughter.
> She will hold him, enfold him, and kiss him.

And yet, in spite of her spirit that nothing can
weaken or dismay, with all her tragic magnificence,
she remains human. Just at the end she says,

> No more blood—
> Oh, if this could be the end. These things I can bear—
> No more.

Aeschylus keeps her human through her power to feel pain, as Shakespeare keeps Macbeth. We know what she has suffered and that she will go on suffering.

There is no character in literature to put beside her. She is Lady Macbeth up to Duncan's murder, and more than Macbeth after it. She can do what she has planned; she did not plan without full justification in her own eyes; remorse will never touch her.

All the other characters, however unimportant beside her, are complete personalities, clearly drawn, with one exception, Clytemnestra's lover. To be sure, he comes in only toward the end, but he does nothing except brag and bluster and threaten the chorus. We would rather have had Clytemnestra facing them alone, our eyes fixed only on her as the curtain falls.

The others, however, are admirable: the watchman on the roof who opens the play, and who gives the first hint of the evil that will grow darker and darker until the end:

> I never close my eyes. Fear is up here, not sleep.
> Singing or whistling help a sleepy man,
> but if I try to make a sound I groan.

The herald, a soldier in every word he speaks, Aeschylus' own experience of war, no doubt, put in his mouth:

> Trouble! If I should tell you how we lived—
> No room on deck and little more below.
> Ashore still worse. Forever rain or dew.
> Our very clothes were rotting from the wet.
> Good for the lice—our hair was full of them.

And Agamemnon, a subtly drawn foil to Clytemnestra, as vain and pompous and weak as she is proud and strongly sure of herself.

Next to her in importance is Cassandra, a strange figure. She had been a princess in Troy and had seen everything ended for her, her people, her home, her city. Besides all else she has had to bear what she calls "the awful pain of prophecy." She is a prophet, never believed, as prophets never are; a little mad, as the inspired often are. At the very end, however, she is only a frightened girl, knowing she must die, ready to die, really, but shrinking from the actual blow, the violence, the pain—a sharp sword in cruel hands.

> I will endure to die. But—pray God the blow strike
> home
> quickly. No struggle. Death coming easily.
> Blood ebbing gently, and my eyes then closed.

The chorus play an important part in the action, as is rare in Greek tragedy, but far more important is what they say in their long choral songs. They tell us what Aeschylus had come to believe in the last years of his life, and sometimes that is quite different from his earlier idea. Two of his plays, the *Persians* and the *Seven Against Thebes*, are full of martial ardor; heroes fight to defend their own; war is glorious. Aeschylus himself had known it at its most glorious; he had fought at Marathon. But in the years between he had learned about war as well as about much else. "To learn is to be young, however old," he makes his chorus of old men say in the *Agamemnon*. He was an old man then himself, but he knew that secret of perpetual youth. He had not stood still at the point where Marathon left him; he never stood still at any point, and he came to look at war in a way which was as unlike Marathon as possible and left it bare of glory. "Economic causes underlie all warfare." He does not put it quite like that, of course.

> Women know whom they sent forth,
> but instead of the living,
> back there come to the house of each
> armor, dust from the burning.
> And War who trades
> men for gold,
> life for death,
> holding scales
> where the spear-points meet and clash—

That figure standing in the midst of the battle fury to weigh coolly in one scale the dead and in the other the money equivalent, is so modern, it might be shown in any anti-war film today, a composite photograph of the business men who promote a war.

It is strange that Aeschylus came to think in that way. He did not watch Athens deteriorate during the war with Sparta, as Euripides did. He died long before, when the Periclean age was in its brilliant beginning, when thirty years of splendid achievement had followed after Marathon. And yet during those years he learned to see war as a business which sent men to die that other men might get rich.

Of course, all through that time there was always fighting going on in this place or that, and Athens had her share in it. She captured here an island and there a town, and the terms she offered can be guessed from the story of what one defender did. He threw his gold and silver into the sea, killed his family and slaves, laid them on a great funeral pyre, and when he had fired it, himself leaped into the flames. Athens must have been horrified. She had so lately dared the loss of everything rather than lose freedom.

Such a story would certainly give Aeschylus matter for meditation, but, one might suppose, it would lead him to paint a picture of war's horrors like Euripides' *The Trojan Women*. He did not do that. He had the sensitiveness and profound feeling of a great poet, but he was a free-thinker, no less. His mind was the kind that perpetually asks, why? What brought war about? He was bent upon that more than upon what war brought about, and he thought his way through the emotionality and excitement and pageantry—cheering crowds, patriotic pride, and all the rest—to what lay hidden far, far beneath, a few quiet men who had made the plan and would make the profits. No one after him saw that for many hundreds of years.

The choral songs of the *Agamemnon* grow more astonishing the more one reads them. Occasionally what they say seems trite, but truisms are truths when they are first discovered, and become trite only because they are so true. But, for the most part, there is no way to appropriate the power of thought and the power of poetry in these songs. They always seem new.

Perhaps—one can never feel certain with a poet like Aeschylus—in a verse in the greatest of them all, he gives his own final belief about the world— that world of which he makes Cassandra say,

> O world of men, what is your happiness?
> A painted show. Comes sorrow and the touch—
> a wet sponge—blots the painting out.

No one ever felt the blackness of the evil always here with us more than he did, and no writing anywhere shows it blacker than the *Agamemnon* does. Nevertheless he did not in the end see it as senseless, signifying nothing. At the very least, he says, this is certain,

> Knowledge won through suffering.
> Drop, drop, in our sleep, upon our hearts,
> sorrow falls, memory's pain,
> and to us, though against our very will,
> even in our own despite,
> comes wisdom,
> by the awful grace of God.

Two hundred years before Aeschylus there lived a Hebrew who would have understood him. The one whom we are constrained to turn to, Isaiah said, is not the radiantly happy, but a man of sorrows and acquainted with grief.

IX

THE *AGAMEMNON*
of AESCHYLUS

⌐⌐⌐

(The scene is laid in Argos before the palace of
AGAMEMNON. *An altar is in the center of the fore-*
ground. On the roof stands a watchman. It is night.)

WATCHMAN

Oh God, for an end to this weary work.
A year long I have watched here, head on arm,
crouched like a dog on Agamemnon's roof.
The stars of night have kept me company.
I know them all, and when they rise and set.
Those that bring winter's cold and summer's heat—
for they have power, those bright things in the sky.
And what I watch for is a beacon fire,*
a flash of flame to bring the word from Troy,
word that the town has fallen.

* In the old stories the Greeks at Troy had arranged to have
a long line of watchmen and fires ready to be lit which would
carry the news from point to point on to Greece whenever
Troy fell.

It's a woman's hope, for a woman is master here,
but her heart is as stout as ever was a man's.
No rest for me by night. I wander up and down.
My bed is wet with dew. Dreams keep away.
Fear is up here, not sleep. I never close my eyes.
Singing or whistling helps a sleepy man,
but if I try to make a sound I groan
for all the evil happenings down there.
Things once were right in this house, but no more.
Oh, for a bit of luck to free me now,
that fire to bring good news out of the night.

> (*A pause. He stands silent, watching. In the dark
> a spark of light is seen. It grows brighter, spread-
> ing into a blaze.*)

A flame! Oh, see! It turns the dark to day.
There'll be dancing now and singing in the town.
Ho there! Ho there! O Agamemnon's Queen,
wake—wake.
Up from your bed— Quick, quick—and shout for
    joy.
Shout for the beacon light. Troy—Troy is taken.
The messenger has come, the fire signal.

> (*Lights and movement are seen within the
> palace.*)

I'll start the dancing up here by myself.
The dice have fallen well. I'll mark the score.
This beacon fire has thrown us three times six.
Oh, let me see my master home again,
and hold once more his dear hand in my own.
Those other things—no more of them. I put
a weight big as an ox upon my tongue.
And yet the very house, if it had voice,

would speak out clear—just as I too speak out
to those who know. To those who do not—why,
I lose my memory.

(*Exit.*)

(*Attendants enter from the palace with torches,
and kindle fire on the altar and sprinkle incense.*
CLYTEMNESTRA *with women in attendance enters
and kneels before the altar. From the side a band
of old men march in. They chant the chorus as
they slowly march around the altar. During the
song the day begins to dawn.*)

CHORUS

The tenth year is this from the time Priam's foe,
the great adversary,
Agamemnon and Prince Menelaus,
with honor of scepter and honor of throne,
strong men, yoked together and brothers,
launched a thousand ships from this Argive land,
a warrior band to carry help,
and they shouted a great shout, War!
So eagles scream as they circle aloft
on their feathered oars,
high over their nest on a lonely crag,
when the eaglets are stolen away.
And they grieve for their young
and the nest never more to be tended.
But in heaven above there is one who hears,
or Pan or Zeus or Apollo,
hears the shrill, screaming cry of the dwellers in air,
and slow-footed vengeance
he sends to those that transgress.

Even thus the Almighty who guards guest and host,
sent the children of Atreus to Paris,
for a woman wooed of many men.
And many a struggle that weighs down the limbs,
when the knee is bowed in the dust,
when the spear-shaft is shivered in the prelude of
      the fight,
he has sent to the Greek and the Trojan.
It is as it is. It shall end as it must.
Not by secret grief, not by secret gifts,
not by tears, can one make atonement
for altars without fire and the stubborn wrath of
      God.
But we, all unhonored for that we are old,
left behind when the host sailed to help,
weak as a child, we lean on our staves.
We are waiting.
When the marrow in the bones is young,
when a child's heart is lord within the breast,
war is far away—the aged are like children.
He that is exceeding old, when the leaf is withered,
walks the roads on three feet with his staff.
No better than a child,
he wanders, a dream—at noonday.
      (*As the old men take their positions around the
      altar, they approach nearer to* CLYTEMNESTRA. *She
      does not appear to notice them.*)
But you, Tyndarus' daughter,
Queen Clytemnestra, what thing is this?
What tidings, what news, has aroused you?
You have sent to the shrines. They have kindled the
      fires,

and the gods that guard the city,
gods of heaven and gods of hell,
gods of the market and gods of the field,
the sacrifice flames on their altars.
From one and another heaven-high
the fire is leaping.
They have brought from the king's treasure holy oil,
thick unguents of myrrh and honey,
to coax the flame with a magic spell,
a pure and guileless persuasion.
Tell us of these things what is known
and what may be spoken.
Heal us now of our fear
that works in us thoughts of evil.
The light from your altars shows us hope,
hope that defends from consuming care,
from grief that eats away life.

(CLYTEMNESTRA *still takes no notice of them but
goes silently into the palace. The marching song,
in Greek tragedy sung as the chorus entered and
took their positions, comes here to an end, and the
chorus proper begins. They sing of the omen
shown to the two leaders of the army,* AGAMEM-
NON *and* MENELAUS, *as they were starting for
Troy—two eagles that tore a hare to pieces.*)

CHORUS

Power is mine to sing of a journey of heroes fate-
    driven.
Old though we are the spirit of God breathes in us
music's mighty persuasion.

How then the two,
the twin-throned strength of the young men of
    Hellas,
two with one purpose,
were sent with spear and with hand to seek venge-
    ance
by a rushing bird to the land of Teucer.
To the kings of ships came the kings of birds, one
    black and the other with tail white-feathered.
By the house of the king,
high toward the spear-hand where all could behold
    them,
two birds swooping together
tore at a pregnant hare and the brood of her young
    big within her.
Forever ended her swift coursing.
Sorrow, sing sorrow, but good shall prevail with
    power.

Calchas the wise, the host's seer, beholding two with
    one spirit,
Atreus' warrior sons, knew them for the eagles,
leaders and captains,
and thus he foretold the omen:
A time shall be
when these shall capture the city of Priam.
Before the towers,
sheep and oxen, the wealth of the people,
the fortune of war will ravage and slaughter.
Only may never our army, the great curb of Troy,
    be foredoomed by the anger of heaven.

For pity and wrath
move in the heart of Artemis * holy.
Winged hounds, eagles of Zeus,
slew a poor cowering creature, her unborn young
  slaughtered with her.
She loathes the feast the eagles made.
Sorrow, sing sorrow, but good shall prevail with
  power.
So gentle is she, loveliest,
to dewy youth,
fierce lions' tender sucklings,
the young of the beasts that roam the meadow,
nurslings of all wild forest creatures,
yet does she ask for the omen's fulfillment,
the signs from heaven, the good and the evil.
But I call upon God the healer,
Let her not send to the Greeks ill winds that will
  hold fast the ships from the sailing,
seeking to lay on her altar a victim abhorrent to
  offer,
worker of strife among kinsmen that spares not and
  fears not to murder.
For terrible, ever up-springing,
treachery waits in the house to avenge the old murder of children.†

 * The huntress and yet the protector too of wild animals. It
was to her that Agamemnon sacrificed his daughter, Iphigenia,
to get favorable winds for the fleet on its way to Troy, when
they had long been weather-bound. Symbolic utterances are, of
course, not marked by clarity. Here the eagles are the two
Greek leaders and the hare is Iphigenia. Then suddenly the
symbol shifts and Artemis is demanding the sacrifice of Iphigenia
—to expiate the death of the hare.
 † Atreus killed the children of Thyestes, his brother, and

These were the words of Calchas. With mightiest
    blessings he spoke them,
omens of fate from the birds on the road to the house
    of the chieftain.
So in accordance,
Sorrow, sing sorrow, but good shall prevail with
    power.

God—who is he? If that name he choose,
by it I will cry to him.
Nothing can I reach in thought,
all things searching to the depths,
nothing save God, if the load of vain care from my
    spirit
I must cast and find the truth.

One first—who was great to them of old,
full of swollen blustering wrath,
now is as a tale that's told.
He who next came, went his way *
like a wrestler overthrown.
God—he who hails him in triumph as victor forever,
shall be led to understand.

Guide of mortal man to wisdom,
he who has ordained the law,
knowledge won through suffering.

served them to him at a banquet in revenge for his having
seduced his wife.
   * Two rulers of the gods preceded Zeus—whom Aeschylus
now calls Zeus and now God and who is to him the supreme
power behind all things, as unlike the Zeus of the myths as possible.

Drop, drop—in our sleep, upon the heart
sorrow falls, memory's pain,
and to us, though against our very will,
even in our own despite,
comes wisdom
by the awful grace of God.

Then the leader of the ships,
prince of all the Grecian host,
spoke no word to blame the seer,
bent beneath
fortune's sudden stroke of doom.
When the ships could not sail, and the food
failed through all the Grecian camp
spread along the Thracian coast,
in Aulis where
waves roar with the ebb and flow.

And from the north
ever blew the storm wind.
It broke men's hearts.
Famine-struck they wandered
away to death.
It wasted ships,
spared not sheet nor cable.
The time dragged,
doubling itself in passing.
The slow delay
withered the flower of Grecian youth.
But when to soothe the storm
a way of bitter evil,
weighting with sorrow the chieftains,

the prophet shrieked forth, calling upon
Artemis, queen,
so that the kings,
striking the ground,
scepter in hand,
could not hold a tear back—

The elder prince
lifted his voice in sorrow:
Heavy my load
if I refuse and obey not.
But heavy too
if I must slay
the joy of my house, my daughter.
A father's hands
stained in dark streams flowing with blood of a girl
slaughtered before the altar.
For me on every side is woe.
How desert my ship-mates?
Traitor to those who are with me?
Justice is with them when they seek
eagerly eager
wild winds to calm
even with blood,
blood of a girl.
And now may good befall us.

But when he bowed beneath the yoke of fortune,
shifting his sails to meet a wind of evil,
unholy, impious, bringing him to dare to think
what should not be thought of—
For men grow bold

when delusion leads them.
A frenzied counselor, that,
source of all sin.
The end—maddened he dared the deed,
slaying his child to help a war
waged for the sake of a woman,
ships to speed in their sailing.

And all her prayers—cries of Father, Father,
her maiden life,
these they held as nothing,
the warrior-judges, battle-mad.
Her father bade
with a prayer to lift her,
like a lamb, high above the altar.
Her garments wrapping her round,
falling forward,
her soul failed. Aloft they raised her,
binding her sweet lips with a curb,
stifling her cry of ill omen,
fraught with a curse to the king's house,
with force of bonds,
silent guards,
muffled might.

Upon the ground
fell her robe of saffron,
and from her eyes
sped an arrow
that pierced with pity those that slew her.
I see her there,
a picture clear before my eyes.

She strives to speak, as oftentimes,
her father near, at the banquet table,
she used to sing, the little maid,
pure voice raised,
honoring her father loved,
while in love
joining her, he poured the wine for blessing.

What then befell I did not see, I do not say.
The prophet's wiles failed not of fulfillment.
The scales of God
weigh to all
justice: those that suffer learn.
What shall be
slow time will show.
Never seek to know before.
Such seeking brings
grief too soon. For shining clear
will it dawn at sunrise.
    (CLYTEMNESTRA, *attended by her women, enters.*)
But now may good
come at last
after ill.
So she prays
who guards alone
this our land, a sure defense to her lord returning.

LEADER OF CHORUS

I come to do you reverence, Clytemnestra.
For it is right to give the king's wife honor,
a woman on a throne a man left empty.
But if you know of good or only hope

to hear of good and so do sacrifice,
I pray you speak. Yet if you will, keep silence.

CLYTEMNESTRA

With glad good tidings, so the proverb runs,
may dawn arise from the kind mother night.
For you shall learn a joy beyond all hope:
the Trojan town has fallen to the Greeks.

LEADER

You say? I cannot hear—I cannot trust—

CLYTEMNESTRA

I say the Greeks hold Troy. Do I speak clear?

LEADER

Joy that is close to tears steals over me.

CLYTEMNESTRA

Quite right. Such tears give proof of loyalty.

LEADER

What warrant for these words? Some surety have
    you?

CLYTEMNESTRA

I have. How not—unless the gods play tricks.

LEADER

A fair persuasive dream has won your credence?

CLYTEMNESTRA

I am not one to trust a mind asleep.

LEADER

A wingless rumor then has fed your fancy?

CLYTEMNESTRA

Am I some little child that you would mock at?

LEADER

But when, *when*, tell us, was the city sacked?

CLYTEMNESTRA

This night, I say, that now gives birth to dawn.

LEADER

And what the messenger that came so swift?

CLYTEMNESTRA

A god! The fire-god flashing from Mount Ida.
Beacon sped beacon on, couriers of flame.
First, Ida signaled to the island peak
of Lemnos, Hermes' rock, and swift from there
Athos, God's mountain, fired the great torch.
It leaped, it skimmed the sea, a might of moving
    light,
joy-bringing, golden shining, like a sun,
and sent the fiery message to Macistus.
Whose towers, then, in haste, not heedlessly
or like some drowsy watchman caught by sleep,
sped on the herald's task and flashed the beacon
afar, beyond the waters of Euripus,
to sentinels high on Messapius' hillside,
who fired in turn and sent the tidings onward,
touching with flame a heap of withered heather.
So, never dimmed but gathering strength, the splen-
    dor
over the levels of Asopus sprang,
lighting Cithaeron like the shining moon,
rousing a relay there of traveling flame.
Brighter beyond their orders given, the guards
kindled a blaze and flung afar the light.

It shot across the mere of Gorgopis.
It shone on Aegiplanctus' mountain height,
swift speeding on the ordinance of fire,
where watchers, heaping high the tinder wood,
sent darting onward a great beard of flame
that passed the steeps of the Saronic Gulf
and blazing leaped aloft to Arachnaeus,
the point of lookout neighbor to our town.
Whence it was flashed here to the palace roof,
a fire fathered by the flame on Ida.
Thus did they hand the torch on, one to other,
in swift succession finishing the course.
And he who ran both first and last is victor.
Such is my warrant and my proof to you:
my lord himself has sent me word from Troy.

LEADER

The gods—oh, I will thank them soon in prayer.
But tell me clearly now once more your tale,
that I may know and wonder—

CLYTEMNESTRA

Troy lies this day in the Achaeans' hands.
I think within the town a great cry rises
that will not blend, as when into a cruse
one pours together oil and vinegar.
Even so the cries of victor and of vanquished,
that differ as their lot is different.
For these have flung themselves on lifeless bodies
of husbands, brothers—little children cling
to the old dead who gave them life and sob
from throats no longer free, above their dearest.
While those—a night of roaming after battle

has set them hungry down to break their fast
on what the town affords, not in due order,
but as each man has drawn his lot by chance.
They are quartered in the captured homes of Troy,
no more beneath the open sky, delivered
from frost and dew, and there like happy men
all night they sleep without a sentinel.
Now, if they keep them clear of guilt to gods,
to shrines within the town and conquered land,
the captors shall not in their turn be captured—
if mad desire fall not on the army,
in greed for gain, to violate the holy.
For still before them lies the second lap
of their long course ere they can win safe home.
And though they wend their way unerringly,
what those dead suffered may yet work them ill,
—that pain * which never sleeps—and fresh woe
      come.
Such words you hear from me that am a woman.
But may good conquer, shining clear to all.
Of many blessings this joy I would choose.

LEADER

Mistress, like some wise man you speak with
      wisdom,
and I who hear you judge your warrant good.
So that I turn to God to offer thanks
for deeds done that are price for all the toil.
      (CLYTEMNESTRA *enters the palace—the* CHORUS
      take their positions for the second choral song.)

* Her own, which never forgets her daughter, sacrificed ten
years ago.

CHORUS

O all-ruling God and bounteous night,
great gifts of glory you bring us.
Who cast over Troy and her towered walls
a close-meshed net none could win way through,
none could leap beyond, never man, never child,
a snare that enslaved,
a doom that caught all in its clutches.
Heaven's Lord, who guards both guest and host,
I worship. These deeds were wrought by him.
Of old against Paris he bent his bow,
and the bolt fell neither short of the mark,
nor passed it, flying star-ward.

The blow God strikes, so say men ever.
They search out him and searching find him.
He wills and it is done. There spoke one saying:
God cares not when
men tread down
holy things inviolate
underfoot.
But who spoke thus
knew not God.
Our eyes have seen the price
the proud must pay in full
for daring deeds beyond man's daring.
When dwellings overflow with riches,
the greatest good
is not there:
wealth enough to keep away
misery,
and hearts that are wise to use it.

Gold is never a bulwark,
no defense to the haughty,
arrogance spurning out of sight
God's great altar of justice.

Temptation,
wickedly persuading,
destruction,
child of scheming mischief,
when they constrain what power can deliver?
No hiding place
covers sin.
It blazes forth
a light of death.
Metal base
when tested shows
black of grain.
A touchstone too is there
that tests men's lives and shows—
a child running after a bird on the wing,
to town and kin
a fool, a shame past bearing.
And if he prays,
no one hears,
not a god.
So too Paris once coming,
entered a friend's kind dwelling,
shamed the hand there that gave him food,
stealing away a woman.

And she—she left
clash of spears,

clang of shields,
to kith and kin,
gifts from her,
armored ships and sailors.
To Troy she brought in place of dower doom and
      death.
So swiftly through the gates did she go
to dare what none must dare. And deep they
      groaned,
the seers within
that house * abandoned, crying:
Alas—alas— A home, a home, the lord thereof.
Alas, a bed
pressed in love by one beloved.
In the house
one may see
silence, all alone,
dishonor borne without rebuke.
He longs for her
beyond the sea.
A ghost holds sway
where she once was mistress.
Beauty grown to him hateful,
grace of fair-fashioned statues.
Empty his eyes for want of her.
Lost all things that are lovely.

In dreams there come,
haunting him,
sweet fancies fond,

* The house of Menelaus, after Helen—his wife—had gone to
Troy with Paris.

vain delight
bringing with them ever.
For vainly when the dreamer thinks to clasp his joy,
the vision slips through his hands and is lost.
It goes, a phantom swift, it vanishes
on wings that move
down the ways of slumber.
Within the house
these sorrows sit upon the hearth.
Nor they alone,
but woes surpassing even these.
For all who sped
forth to Troy,
joining company,
such grief as passes power to bear
in each man's home,
plain to see.
Many things
there to pierce a heart through.
Women know whom they sent forth,
but instead of the living,
back there comes to the house of each
armor, dust from the burning.

And War who trades
men for gold,
life for death,
holding scales
where the spear-points meet and clash,
to their beloved
back from Troy
he sends them dust

from the flame,
heavy dust,
dust wet with tears,
filling urns in seemly wise,
freight well stowed, the dust of men.
They make lament and speak each fair.
This one so wise in battle-lore,
that one fell nobly in the fight
and died—for whom? Another's wife.
So in silence the women speak.
So in secret a jealous pain
creeps toward the sons of Atreus.
Far away lie the victors,
near the walls of the Trojans,
fair young limbs in a hostile land,
foemen's earth for their burying.

A people's voice,
angered sore,
carries dread.
Those they curse,
lost and doomed must pay in full.
But dark fear now
shows me dim
dreadful shapes,
hid in night.
Men who shed the blood of men,
their ways are not unseen of God.
Black the spirits that avenge.
Or late or soon they lay him low
who prospers in unrighteousness.
His life a wavering shadow lost

in the unseen where none may help.
Overmuch fame a peril brings.
Heads carried high God's lightning strikes,
flame from his eyes, all-seeing.
Mine be good free from envy.
Not for me cities captured.
Neither let me a captive be,
holding my life from another.

A SINGLE MEMBER OF THE CHORUS

But tidings glad,
fire-spread,
throughout the town
swiftly go,
whether true or whether false
what man can know? A god, maybe, is tricking us.

ANOTHER

Yes. Who so childish, mind so shattered, that a flame,
a traveling fire
bearing news,
can set his heart
all a-fire, to sink and die
when another tale is told?

ANOTHER

Women we are not,
who before the truth is clear
give their trust to what they will.

ANOTHER

Credulous ever the mind of a woman is, leaping all
    bounds.
So swiftly it moves, so swiftly, too, pass

a woman's words.
News she spreads is short of life.

> (*A break in the action is presupposed here. Several days are assumed to have passed. The chorus of old men have again assembled.*)

LEADER

Now we shall soon have knowledge of these fires,
these beacon-flames, these torches relayed on,
if they bring truth or only like to dreams
glad-seeming, visit us to cheat our sense.
A herald comes. I see him by the shore.
His brow is shaded by an olive-branch.
And, witness to his journey, see the dust,
the thirsty dust, twin-sister to the mire,
that fouls his dress and gives assurance clear
here is no voiceless messenger to speak
by kindling fires of mountain wood, and signs
of flame and smoke, but one who will speak out
and bid us plainly either to rejoice
or else— What else? I will not say the word.
To this of good we see may more good come.

ANOTHER OLD MAN

Let him who prays not thus for land and town
reap in himself the fruit of evil thought.

> (*Enter the* HERALD. *His dress is travel-worn and stained.*)

HERALD

O dear home of my fathers, Argos land!
Ten years have come and gone. This day I see you.

One hope come true of many hopes made shipwreck.
Oh, never did I think to die at home,
to have my share in that dear earth.
Now blessings, blessings on the land, the sun,
the land's most high king, Zeus, and Lord Apollo,
loosing no more against us his keen shafts.
Enough of hate you showed us by Scamander.*
Turn to us as of old, to save and heal.
Gods all, here met, to you I make my prayer.
Hermes, the herald, whom the heralds love,
the sovereign dead who sped us on our way,
kind welcome give these whom the spear has spared.
Oh, palace of our kings, beloved roof,
seats of the mighty, gods that front the sun,
if ever once in days of old, then now
look with glad eyes upon a king who comes
after long lapse of years to bring to you
and all here gathered, light in the dark night.
Receive him with due honor—Agamemnon.
Welcome him as is meet and right to do.
He took the mattock from the hand of Zeus, the just.
With it uprooted Troy, leveled her to a plain.
Dark are her altars, dark her shrines of gods.
The seed has perished out of all the land.
Such is the yoke he put upon Troy's neck,
our king, the elder of the sons of Atreus.
Blest of the gods he comes, the man most fit
of all men now alive to meet with honor.
For neither Paris nor his town that shared
with him his guilt, will ever boasting say

* Apollo was on the Trojan side. The Scamander was one of
the rivers of Troy.

that what they did was more than what they suffered.
Judgment against him given for rape and theft,
his booty lost, he brought to utter ruin
his father's house so that the very place
knows it no more. Twice over Priam's sons
paid for the wrong they did.

LEADER

Oh, herald from the host, we give you joy.

HERALD

Joy truly—such that I could die content.

LEADER

So much you longed for home and fatherland?

HERALD

So much that now my eyes are wet from joy.

LEADER

Homesickness is a pleasant malady.

HERALD

You mean? I cannot master that alone.

LEADER

To long for those who long for you in turn—

HERALD

Our home then missed us who were sick for home?

LEADER

So that our darkened minds could only grieve.

HERALD

But why such weight of sorrow on your heart?

LEADER

Long since I learned that silence physics pain.

HERALD

No—tell me, with the prince gone did you fear?

LEADER

Even as you said: death would be only joy—

HERALD

Well ended now. And yet in those long years
a man might say the evil matched the good.
But who except a god can look to be
free from all trouble all his days on earth.
Trouble! If I should tell you how we lived—
No room on deck, and little more below.
All in the day's work, but we paid for it.
Ashore still worse, whatever men hate most.
Beds in the open, near the foeman's walls.
Forever rain or dew, the meadow dew.
Our very clothes were rotting from the wet.
Good for the lice—our hair was full of them.
The winters—well, if anyone would try
to say how cold it was—the birds fell dead.
And Ida's snow—enough to break your heart.
Hot, too, at noonday when upon his couch
the sea, windless and waveless, lay asleep.
But why complain? All trouble over now.
All over for the dead. They will not want
to live again—not they, never again.
And we who live will let them lie uncounted.
Why grieve now because fortune frowned on them?
A long good-by to trouble, so say I.

For us, we soldiers that are left alive,
the gain and not the loss weighs down the scale.
So that we make our boast to this day's sun,
as swift we fly across the land and sea:
"Troy at last captured, the Achaean fleet
has nailed these spoils of war up in the shrines,
paying the gods of Greece their ancient tribute."
And whoso hears must give the city glory,
the leaders too, and thank God for his grace,
who brought these things to pass. My tale is told.

LEADER

Convinced. I own it. Such words win belief.
To learn is to be young, however old.
But news that makes me rich belongs yet more
to the king's house there—and to Clytemnestra.

   (*As these words are spoken* CLYTEMNESTRA *enters.*)

CLYTEMNESTRA

My triumph song I sang long since, when first
the fire-sped messenger came through the night,
proclaiming Ilium captive and laid low.
Some then spoke to me chiding: Beaconfires—
do these persuade you Troy is spoiled and sacked?
How like a woman, quickly light of heart.
They made me out a fool with wits astray.
Yet did I sacrifice, and everywhere,
throughout the town, one man and then another
followed a woman, joining in her praise,
echoing her triumph, and in all the shrines
they lulled to rest the fragrant spice-fed flames.
And now what need of words from me to you?

The king himself will tell me all the tale.
But that I best may hasten to give welcome
to him, my honored lord, as he returns—
for what so sweet in any woman's eyes,
a lamp in darkness, when, the gates flung wide,
her man, saved by God's grace, comes back from
    war—
take to my lord this message: bid him come
with all the speed he may, back to the town
that loves him, and within his palace find
the faithful wife he left there, through these years
a trusty watch-dog for him in his house,
foe to his foes, not changed in any wise,
on whom he set his seal, unbroken still
in the long lapse of time.
Pleasure from other men, a tarnished name,
these things are not for me. As easily
could I be taught to dye a bit of bronze.
   (*Exit* CLYTEMNESTRA.)

HERALD

Such ringing words when laden with the truth
are not amiss in a true woman's mouth.

LEADER

Spoken for your ears, not for ours.
We are interpreters that understand too well.
But, herald, tell us, what of Menelaus?
Has he won home in safety, come with you?
A strong man he, one whom this land loves well.

HERALD

There is no way to tell a pleasant falsehood
whose pleasure will endure as the days pass.

LEADER

Good news if true—if not true then not good.
Evil when true is hard to cover up.

HERALD

Swept away out of sight of all the fleet,
he and his ship. I do not speak a lie.

LEADER

You saw him, then, set sail? or was he lost
in some great storm that threatened all the ships?

HERALD

O master-bowman, you have hit the mark.
One word or two and all our trouble told.

LEADER

Do sailors speak of him as dead or living?
What do men say who travel on the sea?

HERALD

Not a man knows, not one to bring clear tidings.
He only saw, who quickens earth—the sun.

LEADER

How rose, how passed, the storm? The gods were
    angered?

HERALD

This day of happy omen let no tongue
that tells of evil, darken. Far apart
keep sorrow and the service due to God.
Of course, when to a town a grim-faced messenger
brings fearful tidings of an army fallen,
one common wound for all the folk to suffer,
and many men from many homes made victims

to the two-handled scourge the war-god loves,
a curse that points two ways, a bloody pair—
why then, a man packed full of such like troubles
will make his cry to hell and not to heaven.
But when one comes to bring his happy town
glad tidings of good peace, and safety won,
why mix the evil with the good?
Shall I tell you of the storm God's anger sent us?
For fire and sea took oath together, they
of old most bitter foes, and proved their bond
in ruin dealt the wretched ships of Argos.
At night a bitter evil of cruel waves
uprose and from the north the winds swept down.
Ship shattered against ship, so furiously
that evil shepherd, the wild hurricane,
drove them with roar of rain and thundering spray,
away—unseen—forever gone.
And when uprose the shining light of day
the sea had blossomed—on it floated thick
the flower of our host among the wreckage.
Ourselves, our ship, safe, not a timber sprung.
Someone, a god, no human, took the helm;
stole us away or begged us off from death.
Good Fortune boarded us, a willing shipmate.
Our anchor held against the foaming surf
that could not dash us on the rocky coast.
Saved from that hell of waters, when at last
the white day dawned it was beyond belief
we lived. Our darkened minds saw this alone,
this last calamity, the fleet shipwrecked.
Does one of them still draw the breath of life?
Then he is saying we are lost—why not?

As we in turn think it is so with them.
Good luck be with them. But for Menelaus,
look to see him returning first of all,
if anywhere a ray of sunshine finds him
alive and seeing the sweet light. God's plan.
Be sure he is not minded yet to bring the race to
        ruin.
There still is hope the prince will come back home.
Hearing these words, know that you hear the truth.
        (*Exit* HERALD. *The* CHORUS *take their position for
        another choral song.*)

CHORUS

Who was he who gave her name,*
name so fearfully made true.
Was it one no man may see,
power dread,
knowing what had been foredoomed,
tongue that destiny controlled?
Calling her Helen, bride of strife,
bride of the spear—the spear she wielded.
Through the ships, through men, through her town
        she drove it.
Forth she stepped from her bower,
from the costly, broidered hangings,
by a mighty wind borne sea-ward.
And a host,
shield-bearing huntsmen, followed hot,
tracking the oar blades unseen footprints,

---

* A Greek word that means to destroy has the same sound as
Helen's name. Obviously Hell is the English equivalent of the
pun. But I prefer not to use it, even at the expense of fidelity.
Hell seems nowadays to lack dignity.

on to Simois' * shaded strand.
Oarsmen beached a boat there.
Blood was to flow in that quarrel.

Wrath of God that works his will
sped to Ilium a bride,
curse they called her when they knew,
when they paid
price in full for hearth defiled,
wrong to God who guards the hearth.
Singing aloud the marriage song
came they to honor bride and bridal,
upon whom the charge of the music lay,
near kin to the bridegroom.
But another song was taught them,
taught the ancient Trojan city,
and she groaned,
mourning in desolation deep
him who had sought the fatal bridal.
Desolation forevermore
dying children brought her,
blood that must flow to no purpose.

A man captured a lion's cub,
nursing still at its mother's breast,
reared it then in his dwelling.
Soft little thing in life's prelude,
gentle and fond of the children,
plaything the old took delight in,
holding it often in their arms,
fondling it like a little child.

* The Simois was a river of Troy.

Bright-eyed creature, it licked the hand
giving food for its hunger.

A day came when the lion cub
paid his price for the fostering care,
showed the strain he was bred from,
turning to kill in the sheep-folds.
Banquet unbidden he made him.
Blood in the court-yards was flowing,
anguish past bearing in the house,
slaughter and ruin far and wide.
Priest of death by the wrath of God,
death to those that had reared him.

So once there came
to the town of Ilium
what seemed
a very dream of peace,
the calm no wind stirs ever,
a rich man's
fragile, shining jewel,
soft eyes that glancing shot a dart,
flower of love that pierced men's hearts.
But she swerved sharp and she worked out
to a bitter end her bridal.
In her house base, to her friends base,
and she brought doom where she entered.
God—he avenged whom she wronged,
that bride of tears and accursèd.

An ancient word,
fashioned long ago by men,

speaks thus:
When prosperity
spreading waxes mighty,
it dies not
childless but leaves offspring.
Over much good grows rank apace,
evil crop for the race's reaping.
But alone I in my thought stand
and apart hold I from others.
It is sin only that breeds sin,
and the son is like to the father.
Blest house that harbors the good,
fairest sons are her portion.

But arrogance,
once grown old,
brings to birth
arrogance,
in the miseries of men
forever young. Her day of birth, or late or soon,
is fixed by fate.
Bold recklessness is her twin, irresistible,
none may wage war with, impious.
Curses to home and hearth,
black—like to the one who bore them.

But goodness shines,
giving light, in smoke-begrimed
hovels dim,
virtue there in honor held.
From gilded roofs that cover hands defiled with sin
she turns her eyes.

Where purity dwells, there she betakes herself.
Power of wealth she worships not,
counterfeit glory men love.
All to their haven guiding.

> (*Enter* AGAMEMNON *in a chariot.* CASSANDRA *follows in another. Attendants, soldiers, townsmen. During the* CHORUS' *speech of welcome,* CLYTEMNESTRA, *with attendants, comes through the palace doors and stands on the steps.*)

CHORUS

Come at last, O my king! Troy town is your spoil,
true son of your race.
How shall I greet you, how do you homage,
not over-passing, not falling short of,
    due measure of praise.
Full many there are who give honor first
to fair seeming—the truth they regard not.
To heave a sigh when another fares ill,
    all men are minded.
    Sorrow that bites deep—
    never a pang
    reaches their heart's core.
And joy is feigned in the joy of a friend,
while a long-drawn face is constrained to smile.
But he who is wise to discern his flock,
    a shepherd of men,
    looks into false eyes and there finds
foul that seemed fair, and for friendship
    adulation,
    not wine but water.
When you marshaled the host in Helen's behalf,

through those days as I watched—
frank words be mine now—
dark were the colors that painted your portrait then.
A helmsman that could not steer his own mind,
   such a one as would bring
   boldness in vain *
   while men lay dying.
Now deep from my heart and my heart's deepest
   love

   .   .   .   .

Glad end can make toil to seem merry.
Time, wisest of teachers, will guide you to know
him who dealt justly, him who did evil,
of the men who guarded the town here.

AGAMEMNON
First Argos and my country's gods I greet,
as is their due who helped with me to bring
the host safe home and with me dealt out justice
to Priam's town. No ear to prayer or plea
did the gods give; not one whit wavering
they cast their votes into the urn of blood
for death, to Ilium and all therein.
The other urn, the merciful, was empty,
no hand to fill it, only hope stood by.
The smoke still shows where once a city was.
The whirlwind of blind doom is still alive.
From dying embers comes a breath of incense,
rich fragrance of the riches burning there.
Be mindful then of what you owe the gods

* MSS. readings quite uncertain here—and make little sense.
A gap in the MSS. follows.

whose was the deed, when close about the town
we set our snares of wrath for Helen's sake.
The beast of Argos—him the wooden horse
gave birth to—set his teeth into his prey
and ground the town to powder. High they leaped,
that host of shield-armed men. The time of year
was near the setting of the Pleiades.
Over the towered walls a lion sprang
that fed on flesh of men and lapped his fill
of blood of kings.
Thus to the gods I speak first, as is due.
Now, touching you, I heard and bear in mind
your words just spoken, and to all you said
I give assent. I am your advocate.
Few are the men to whom this is inborn,
to give full honor to a friend's good fortune.
But ill will settles on the heart, a poison,
and he who thus grows sick has double burdens,
a heavy heart for his own miseries
and grief to see the blessings of another.
I speak who know, for deeply I have learned
what friendship is—the semblance in a mirror,
a shadow's ghost—when men have seemed to be
all loyalty. Odysseus only—he
who sailed against his will—when once in harness,
pulled with me, proved a faithful yoke-fellow.
Alive or dead, this is his due from me.
All else that bears upon the State, the gods,
we will consider in full conclave, there
appointing general councils of the people.
Where all goes well, to see that it endures.
Whatever needs a healing remedy,

give care that by kind use of knife or cautery
the mischief of the taint may be averted.
Now to my palace, to my home,
my hearth, where first the gods shall have my greet-
    ing,
who sent me forth and led me back again.
O Victory, now mine, be mine forever.
    (CLYTEMNESTRA *descends the steps of the palace
    followed by her waiting-women.*)

CLYTEMNESTRA

My country-men, chief elders of our city,
it does not shame me to speak out to you
the love I bear my husband. Timid fears
die in us with long lapse of time.
I have not learned from others. No—I speak
of my own life, bitter to bear, the while
he lay beneath the walls of Ilium.
A woman sits at home—a man goes forth.
She first of all knows loneliness and terror,
forever giving ear to angry rumor.
First comes one messenger, then comes another,
and each with tidings worse than were the last,
shrieking calamity to house and household.
If he who now stands here had met with wounds
as many as report came pouring in,
no network were as full of holes as he.
If he had died the deaths they told to me—
so went the tale most often—separate bodies,
three at the least, like Geryon of old,
he would have needed, and a triple share
of earth for covering he must have claimed,

each body dying in a separate death.
Such tidings ever reaching me afresh,
so drove me on that others oftentimes
have loosed the tight-drawn halter from my neck.
And that is why the boy is not here with me,
as he should be, Orestes, in whom met
the pledges of our love. But do not think it strange.
One rears him who has raised his spear for you
in all good will, the Phocian Strophius.
He gave me warning of a twofold trouble,
your danger by the walls of Ilium,
and if the people so left leaderless,
a noisy rabble, should destroy the council.
For men are thus, they trample on the fallen.
Such is our nature—such excuse we plead.
But for myself—the river of my tears
has long run dry—not a drop left to me.
Through the sad watches of the night my eyes
grew dim with weeping, while the fires lit
against your coming ever died unheeded.
The light hum of the buzzing gnat would wake me
from dreams where I had seen more woes to you
than could be suffered in the time I slept.
Such griefs I bore. But now, heart freed from grief,
I speak to him himself who is our safety,
the watch-dog of the fold, the stout ship's forestay,
the firm-based pillar of the lofty roof,
dear as the only son is to his father,
as land the sailor sees beyond his hope,
as day most fair to look on after storm,
to thirsty wayfarer a gushing stream.
Oh, sweet escape from stern necessity.

Thus do I greet him, name him, without fear
the gods may grudge my joy, so many sorrows
I bore of old. Now to me, dear beloved.
Down from your car—but not on common earth
shall your foot rest, my king, the foot that trod
Troy into dust. You women, to your task.
Why this delay? Cover the ground before him
as I gave order. Spread fair tapestries.
Straightway with purple let his path be paved.
—So justice lead him to a home unlooked for.
The rest my care that never sleeps will order
justly, with God and with fate's just decree.

> (*The women cover with purple stuffs the path
> from the chariot to the palace door.* AGAMEMNON
> *does not move.*)

AGAMEMNON

Daughter of Leda, guardian of my house,
long as my absence was so is your speech.
Nor is it seemly you should speak my praise.
Let other lips give me the honor due me.
And these things here—I will not be tricked out
in woman fashion. I am not foreign-bred
that you should grovel on the ground before me
with wide-mouthed noisy praise.
Cover my path—that would draw down upon me
God's jealousy, to whom alone belongs
such honor. For a mortal man to walk
on costly fineries is cause for dread.
I tell you, honor me as man, not god.
Foot rugs and fripperies—away with them.
Fame cries aloud of her own self. The gift

God gives the best is soberness of mind.
Count that alone a happy life which ends
while dear prosperity abides. If I
so fare in all things, courage will not fail me.

CLYTEMNESTRA

Tell me but this—if not against your will—

AGAMEMNON

My will, be sure, shall never be gainsayed.

CLYTEMNESTRA

Is it perhaps some vow fear drove you to?

AGAMEMNON

What I have said I mean if ever man did.

CLYTEMNESTRA

Would Priam so have done, had he been victor?

AGAMEMNON

I do believe he would have walked on purple.

CLYTEMNESTRA

While you stand off, afraid what men may say—

AGAMEMNON

Ah, well—what men say is a mighty power.

CLYTEMNESTRA

The man who stirs no ill will, stirs no envy.

AGAMEMNON

A woman—and so eager for a fight!

CLYTEMNESTRA

To yield would well become a happy victor.

AGAMEMNON

You too would be a victor? Over me?

CLYTEMNESTRA

Yes. Yield to me—but of your own free will.

AGAMEMNON

Well, have your way. Here then, my hunting
    boots—
they did my feet good service—one of you,
quick, draw them off. And as I walk upon
this purple of the sea, may no far stroke
flashed with the jealous eye of God light on me.
    (*He grumbles to himself while his boots are
    drawn off.*)
I hold it shame to waste the house's substance
by putting foot on stuffs that cost much silver.
    (*As he resigns himself to the inevitable, it occurs
    to him that the moment is a propitious one to in-
    troduce an awkward subject,* CASSANDRA.)
Enough of that. This girl you see, a stranger,
take her within, and kindly. He who rules
with gentleness, God looks upon with favor.
A slave's yoke no one bears of his own will.
She, chosen out of many goods and captives,
the flower of all, is mine—the army's gift.
Now, since you have subdued me to your will,
treading on purple I pass to my home.
    (*He descends from the chariot and standing on
    the purple waits for her a moment.*)

CLYTEMNESTRA

There is the sea—and who shall drain it dry?
—breeding in plenteousness and ever fresh

the purple dye men weigh out silver for.
Our house, thank God, has ample store of all,
and poverty it does not understand.
Purple enough I would have vowed to trample
beneath my feet if so the oracles
had bade me as a price for your return.
If the root lives, the tree will put forth green,
shade to the house against the dog-star's heat.
Even so you, coming back to hearth and home,
are sign that warmth has come in wintertime.
And when Zeus makes the wine from the sharp
    grape,
coolness is in the house where through the halls
the rightful lord once more goes in and out.

    (*He turns and walks to the palace and enters it.
    She follows him as far as the doors. Just when she
    is about to go in she stops and breaks into a brief
    intense prayer, as if she had forgotten that anyone
    was near.*)

God, God, fulfillment is with thee. Fulfill
my prayer. That which shall be fulfilled
in Thy care rests.

    (*She goes into the palace.*)

CHORUS

Why for me so steadfastly
hovers still this terror dark
at the portals of my heart prophetic?
Omen of evil I cry, all unbought and unbidden.
Cast it forth, a murky dream?
Ah, but throned within my heart
fear abides,

boldness fails,
faith that wins assurance broken.
  Time has grown old,
sand is heaped on cables cast
where they bound
ships to shore,
when the host put in from sea,
rushing on to Ilium.

Home they come. Mine eyes have seen.
  Other witness need I none.
Yet my heart, self-taught, within sings dirges.
Spirit of vengeance, your music is sung to no lyre.
Happy confidence of hope
once was mine, it fades and dies.
Heart that throbs,
breast that swells,
tides of pain that shake the spirit,
are you but fools?
Nay, you presage what shall be.
Yet I pray
these my words
be as lies that fall to naught,
never to fulfillment come.

Truly say men
nothing is sure.
Sickness or health—
they are neighbors.
Thin is the wall in between.
Ships holding their course yet are driven
where hides the reef. So fate sends

shipwreck to many a man unlooked for.
　　Of the ship's load heave a part
overboard—the ship may live.
Cast away with measured aim
from the gathered wealth within,
all the house shall not go down
over-weighed, and sink the hull.
Famine comes, but the furrows are sown,
and the year will bring forth from God's bounteous
　　　　store-house
gifts which stay the hunger pain.

But if once blood
fall to the ground,
dark tide of death,
it is ended.
Charms are there, magical spells,
to call back, to make live, what was murdered?
　　　*　　.　　　.　　　.　　　.　　　.　　　.

Fate by fate God balances;
doom is crossed by other doom,
so ordained that each gives place.
Thus I muse, or else my thought
would outstrip my tongue to speak
what now whispers in the dark,
grief deep-piercing the heart without hope.
All too late is it now to unweave what is woven.
How see clear with mind aflame?
　　　(*As the choral song ends*, CLYTEMNESTRA *enters.*
　　　She looks toward the chariot where CASSANDRA *is*
　　　still seated.)

* The MS. reading is here confused.

CLYTEMNESTRA

Down now and go within. To you I speak, Cas-
    sandra,
since to this house God in his grace has brought you,
where you may share his sacred rite and stand
with many another slave beside his altar
who is the guardian of all we own.
Down from the car—and be not over-proud.
Even Alcmena's son,* so goes the tale,
in days of long ago was sold and swallowed
the slaves' black bread. And, if one is a slave,
it is well to serve in an old family,
long used to riches. Every man
who reaps a sudden harvest past his hope,
is savage to his slaves beyond the rule.
From us expect such use as custom grants.

    (CASSANDRA *seems to hear nothing. The old men
      of the chorus look pityingly at her and one of
      them speaks to her gently.*)

OLD MAN

It was to you she spoke. Her words are clear.
Now fate has caught you fast within her web.
Yield then, if yield you can. Not yet—not yet?

CLYTEMNESTRA

Unless her speech is some strange foreign tongue
silly as swallows' twittering, my words
must reach her mind and move her to obey.

ANOTHER OLD MAN

Go. What she bids is best. So stands the thing.
Obey her. Leave the chariot's high seat.

   * Hercules.

CLYTEMNESTRA

There she sits fast. I have no time to waste
on such. Even now before the central hearth
the sheep stand ready for the sacrifice,
 (*She speaks with rising anger.*)
—such joy as never did we hope to have.
You there, if you would have a part, make haste.
Have you no wit to catch my meaning? Speak.
If not with words, a gesture—like barbarians.

LEADER

The strange maid needs some plain interpreter.
She trembles like a wild thing newly caught.

CLYTEMNESTRA

Quite mad. Her crazy thoughts are all she hears.
She has not learned—her town but lately captured—
to brook the curb yet. She must foam and bleed
and wear away her passion. Well—I go.
I will not waste more words to be defied.
 (*She enters the palace.*)

ANOTHER OLD MAN

No anger in me, I so pity her.
Poor thing, dismount. Come. Yield to what you
  must.
Take up your strange yoke now and carry it.
 (CASSANDRA *moves slowly down from the chariot.*
 She is dressed as a priestess. She seems not aware
 of the presence of the old men.)

CASSANDRA

Oh, God, God! Apollo—Apollo—

ANOTHER

Why do you cry to him in misery?
Apollo gives no heed to those who mourn.

CASSANDRA

Oh, God, God! Apollo, Apollo!

ANOTHER

Again she cries dark words of evil omen
to him who has no place where sorrow is.

CASSANDRA

Apollo, Apollo, our guide,
guiding me
on to death.
Twice hast thou ruined me—now utterly.

ONE MAN

(*softly to the rest of the* CHORUS.)
Some prophecy of her own fate she speaks.
The thing within that is divine abides,
though in a slave.

CASSANDRA

Apollo, Apollo, our guide,
guiding me
on to death.
Where have you brought me—and to what a house—

ANOTHER

The house of Atreus' sons. What you would know
it is I will tell you, and will tell you true.

CASSANDRA·

No—but a house God hates,
Murders and strangling deaths.

Kin striking down kin. Oh, they kill men here.
House that knows evil and evil—the floor drips red.

ANOTHER
(*aside to the rest.*)

A hound on scent of blood, this stranger girl.
I think that she will find the thing she seeks.

CASSANDRA

Witness! The children cry,[*]
crying for wounds that bleed.
On—on they are leading me. I must go.
A father feasted—and the flesh his children's.

ANOTHER

We knew your strange prophetic power.
Prophets— Ah me. It is not such we need.

CASSANDRA

O God— O God— What would they bring to pass?
Is there a woe that this house knows not?
So great, so great the evil they would bring to pass.
Oh, dark deed, that love hates, beyond cure, beyond
      hope,
—and help stands far away.

ANOTHER

Such prophesyings pass my skill. What first
she spoke, I know—the whole town rings with it.

CASSANDRA

O woman, this—this is it you would do?
He who has lain in your bed, your lord?
The bath to cheer him—then— How tell the end?

[*] She is speaking of the. children Agamemnon's father had killed and served to their father, his brother, to eat.

So swift—see—it comes now. A hand there—a hand
    gropes.
Now—now—another hand—

ANOTHER
Not one word yet to clear my mind. First riddles,
then misty oracles—and not a clue.

CASSANDRA
Oh, look— Oh, terrible.
There—it is coming clear.
Net?—Net of death? Oh, truly.
The snare is she who lies with him. The blood—
it stains her too.
Furies who haunt the house,
shout, for your prey is here.
Death is due.
Doomed is he.

LEADER
What is this fury that you bid cry out
against the house? Such words bring me no cheer.
Back to my heart the blood
surges in fear pale as death.
    So fade
blood-drops ebbing slow,
    when they drip
where is a mortal wound,
    when the light
dims as life sinks low.
    Swift comes death.

CASSANDRA
What? What? Oh see— Oh see.

Hold the bull back—his mate
strikes— Black the horn that gores him.
In a tangle of raiment she caught him. Oh, cunning
    craft!
He falls— The bath— Water is all around,
but it is red— Oh, blood!
    Doom, ah, doom.
This is truth.

LEADER

I do not boast great skill in oracles,
but these things spell some mischief, to my mind.
And truly what of good
ever do prophets bring to men?
Craft of many words,
only through
evil your message speaks.
    Seers bring aye
terror, so to keep
men afraid.

CASSANDRA

Alas, alas! Oh, sad fate.
Poor woman— It is I.
Yes, it is I myself.
My pain that brims the cup.
This place—why did you bring me here? Oh, pity.
Only to die, to die, and not alone.

ANOTHER OLD MAN

Now is she mad of mood and by some god possessed.
Her words—wild they ring,
as for her fate she mourns. So wails
ever the bird with wings of brown,

musical nightingale,
crying O, Itys, child,
lost to me, lost. In grief alone
rich, poor bird.

CASSANDRA

Ah me, ah me, her fate—sweet
melodist, singing bird.
They gave her wings, the gods.
They gave her life unmarred
by tears—sweet life.* While I—for me there waits
a sword, sharp, sharp, that cuts, that cleaves apart—

LEADER

Whence does it come, this woe, on-rushing, borne
    of God,
yet vain—anguish vain.
Terror you cry—ill-omened cry,
fearful, and yet a melody,
        music high,
            rings the strain.
Path that you follow, how
know you its bounds? Oh, ill
bodes your prophecy.

CASSANDRA

Oh bridal, bridal—death
dealing to Paris and Paris' kin.
Scamander's stream,
waters my fathers drank,
once on your bank a girl,

* Cassandra's view of the nightingale cannot be harmonized
with that of the chorus, although scholars have tried. One must
bear in mind always that the MSS. of the AGAMEMNON have come
down to us in very bad shape.

sorrow-doomed, was reared,
tenderly cherished there.
Now to the river loud of lamentation,
the shores of pain, I go to prophesy.

LEADER

What is this word that you speak,
word that is all too clear,
word to a new-born babe
   clear as day.
   Oh, sharp
   sorrow smites my heart,
   while your pain,
   bitter pain,
thrills as a sorrowful song,
   breaking the heart to hear.

CASSANDRA

Oh, heavy-laden town,
worn unto death, unto death brought low.
Oh, dumb beasts slain,
offered to save her walls.
Many the flocks and herds
brought from pasture lands.
Nothing could they avail.
The town must suffer even as it has.
And this hot heart of mine must soon *—

LEADER

Dark upon dark are your words.
New ill that follows old.
Oh—swiftly on you sweeps an evil thing,

* MSS. unintelligible here.

crushing, weighing down,
  calling forth your cry,
  cry of death.
Desolate, weeping, you go.
Never the end see I.

CASSANDRA

Now do I swear no more behind a veil
my truth shall hide like a new-wedded girl.
A shining wind shall blow strong to the sunrise,
and like a breaking wave lift to the light
something far greater than this pain of mine.
No longer will I speak in riddling words.
Be you my witnesses as I search out,
close on the scent, the trail of grievous things
in days long since.
For this house—ever through it sounds a chant
as of a choir singing with one voice,
not good to hear, a chant of evil words.
Drunken with blood, men's blood, to dare the more,
a band of revellers abides within,
of sister Furies—none may cast them out.
So seated in the house a song they sing,
of that first deed of wrong, and one by one
they spurn a brother's bed defiled * and him
who used it. Has my arrow missed or found
the mark? Prophet am I of lies, a babbler
from door to door? Give me your oath in witness
that I know this house, its evils old in story.

AN OLD MAN

An oath you ask—a bond in honor bound?

* When Agamemnon's father seduced his brother's wife.

wrong.

No help there. Yet I marvel that one bred
beyond the sea, of foreign speech, should know
the truth as though her very eyes had seen it.

CASSANDRA

Apollo gave to me my prophet spirit.

ANOTHER

A god—and he desired you? Could that be?

CASSANDRA

Time was I held it shame to speak of it.

ANOTHER

Ah yes. Such feelings are for happy people.

CASSANDRA

He wrestled with me and his breath was sweet.

ANOTHER

You came to the getting of children as is fit?

CASSANDRA

I swore to yield. I lied. I cheated him.

ANOTHER

But you had then the gift of prophecy?

CASSANDRA

And told my people all the woe to come.

ANOTHER

A god—and did not smite you in his wrath?

CASSANDRA

He did. I sinned—and no man more believed me.

ANOTHER

To us you seem to speak the truth indeed.

CASSANDRA

It comes—it comes. Oh, misery.
The awful pain of prophecy—it comes,
a whirling wind of madness.
See them—those yonder by the wall—there—there—
so young—like forms that hover in a dream.
Children they seem—murdered by those they loved.
And in their hands is flesh— It is their own.
And inward parts— Oh, load most horrible.
I see it—and their father made his feast—
Vengeance, I say, from these is shaping still—
a lion's shape,* who never fights, who lurks
within a bed, until the master comes—
The master? Mine. The slave's yoke. I must bear it.
Lord of the ships who laid waste Ilium—
and yet not know that she-wolf's tongue.
She licks her lord's hand—fawns with pricking
      ear,
and bites at last, like secret death.
Such daring has a woman to kill a man?
How name her? Evil beast, a snake,
the monster crouching on the shore to prey on
      sailors,
the mother of hell, mad-raging, wild to war,
implacable, against her very own.
Her cry of joy—oh, woman daring all things,
joyful as men shout when the battle turns.
Her show of triumph for his home-coming—
Believe or not. Why do I longer care?
The thing that is to be shall be. And you

* She means Clytemnestra's lover. He is the son of the man
who was made to feast on his own children.

here standing, soon will in your pity call me
a prophet all too true.

LEADER

How once a father feasted on his children,
those words I understand, cold to my heart.
And terror holds me when she speaks no fancies
but what I know. All else she says I hear—
no more, I have no clue.

CASSANDRA

Then hear the truth.
Your eyes shall look on Agamemnon dead.

AN OLD MAN

Peace, wretched girl. Hush on your lips those words.

CASSANDRA

No peace is on my lips.

ANOTHER

If it must be—O God, not so—not so.

CASSANDRA

You pray. Their care is death.

ANOTHER

Who? Who is he who plots this cursèd thing?

CASSANDRA

You will not read my prophecy aright.

ANOTHER

Because I know the deed could not be done.

CASSANDRA

And yet I speak the Greek tongue—all too well.

ANOTHER

Greek are the oracles but none can read them.

CASSANDRA

Oh, strange! A flame—moving— It comes upon me.
Oh, terrible! Apollo! I see—I see—
A lioness—that walks upon two feet—
a wolf she lies with, the royal lion gone.
It is she will kill me. Pity me.
She brews a poison, and she swears
the vial of her wrath holds death for me.
I too must die because he brought me hither.
Her plan—and while she whets her sword for him.
Why then these gaudy things on head and throat?
They mock at me—the prophet's wreaths—the staff.
Down with you—now, before I die myself. Begone.
   (*She tears off the adornments that mark her a
   prophet, and stamps on them.*)
You fall, and I myself shall follow soon.
Make rich in woe some other woman now.
See now. It is Apollo who has stripped me,
taken his prophet's robe. He watched while I was
      mocked,
still in his livery, reviled by friends
turned foes—one voice—no reason—to them all,
calling me vagrant, mountebank, a cheat,
a beggar. Wretched and starving I endured.
The prophet now has done with me, his prophet.
It is he has brought me to this pass of death.
They slew my father on an altar stone.
For me a block waits hot with murdered blood.
Surely we shall not die unmarked of God.

Another * to avenge will come in turn,
to slay the one who bore him, to exact
blood for a father's blood. A wanderer,
outcast from home, he shall return at last
and crown the sins that blindly doomed his race.
A great oath has been sworn of God most high.
The fallen helpless corpse shall lead him home.
But I—why weep and pity such as these?
I, who once saw the town of Ilium
fare as she fared. And they that cast her down
have thus their end in the decrees of God.
So now I go to end as they have done.
I will endure to die. O gates of death,
my greeting. But—pray God, the blow strike home
quickly. No struggle. Death coming easily.
Blood ebbing gently and my eyes then closed.

LEADER

O woman, full of sorrows, full of wisdom,
you have spoken much. But if in very truth—
if death you see, how can you unafraid
go toward it like a dumb beast to the altar,
driven by the power of God?

CASSANDRA

There is no help, my friends, not any more.

AN OLD MAN

Yet he who dies last in some sort dies best—

CASSANDRA

The day is come. Small gain to me in flight.

* Orestes, who in the play following this returns and kills
Clytemnestra, his mother, because she killed his father.

ANOTHER

Steadfast in pain, O woman brave of heart.

CASSANDRA

None who are happy ever hear such praise.

ANOTHER

A brave death can make happy one who dies.

CASSANDRA

My father, you were brave, and brave your sons.
 (*She moves toward the palace but starts back.*)

ANOTHER

What thing is there? What terror turns you back?

CASSANDRA

Oh, horror—

ANOTHER (*frightened and angry.*)

That cry— Within your own mind is the horror.

CASSANDRA

Death breathing from the doors—blood, drop by
    drop—

ANOTHER (*also angrily.*)

How not? They are sacrificing at the hearth.

CASSANDRA

A breath as from a grave. . . .

ANOTHER (*remonstrating.*)

The costly Tyrean incense! That? No, no.

CASSANDRA

Yet I am going, there within the house to weep
my own and Agamemnon's doom.

I have lived my life. Oh, friends, my terror is not
    vain.
I am no silly bird that fears each bush.
When I am dead bear witness I spoke truth,
when a woman shall lie dead for me,* a woman,
and a man fall for a man who had an evil wife.
So I who am to die beg of your friendship.

OLD MAN

Oh wretched, those whom God tells what shall be.

CASSANDRA

One last word more—but not to sing my dirge.
O sun, O shining light
I shall not see again, I pray to you:
When they who murdered pay for what they did,
let them remember too this thing they did,
this easy thing, to kill a slave, a woman.
O world of men, what is your happiness?
A painted show. Comes sorrow and the touch—
a wet sponge—blots the painting out.
And this moves pity, sadder still than death.
    (*She enters the palace, and the* CHORUS *take their
    places for another song.*)

CHORUS

All unsatisfied are the hearts of men.
No house so great, when fortune comes knocking,
none so well-filled, the door
    bolted and barred,
    warns her away:
    "Enter no more. Enough."

---

* The woman she means is Clytemnestra and the man is her
lover who will also be killed by Orestes.

So to the king did the high gods allow
to lay low Priam's town.
    And he came
    blest with honor of heaven.
Yet—if for the blood
shed in the years gone,
full price he must pay and must die for the dead
so that others who die may have vengeance—
Is there mortal hearing these things who will boast
fate gave him life
safe from all sorrow?
    (*A sudden cry from the palace.*)

VOICE

God! I am struck! My death blow. Here! Within—

LEADER

Silence. A cry. Who is it done to death?

VOICE

O God! Again— Struck down again.

LEADER

Done the deed. That voice—I know it. He who cried
    out was the king.
Now stand close and plan together. Safety. . . . Is
    there any way . . .
    (*The old men gather and debate confusedly.*)

FIRST SPEAKER

I give you straight my judgment. Sound the call.
All citizens to the palace to give aid.

ANOTHER

No, no. Quick action now. Break in at once.
Before they drop the dripping sword, convict them.

ANOTHER

Yes. Some such plan. I give my vote to that.
Action and quick. No time now for delay.

ANOTHER

As clear as day. The first step to their goal
to make themselves the masters of the state.

ANOTHER

While we wait here—wait till they trample down
all that would hold them back. Their hands are
    quick.

ANOTHER

If I knew what to say—what plan to urge—
Let those give counsel who have strength to act.

ANOTHER

So I think too. There are no words I know
to make the dead arise and live again.

ANOTHER

What? Drag our lives out in submission? Yield
to rulers who have brought pollution on us?

ANOTHER

Intolerable. Far better let us die.
Death is a milder master than a tyrant.

ANOTHER

We have no witnesses. A groan we heard.
We are not seers to know the man is dead.

ANOTHER

Clear facts first—then grow angry as we will.
But guesswork is another thing from knowledge.

LEADER

We are agreed on this at least, to know
and quickly, what has happened to the king.

*(As they press toward the door of the palace it
opens. The bodies of* AGAMEMNON *and* CASSANDRA
lie just within. CLYTEMNESTRA *stands over them.
Blood stains are on her face and dress.)*

CLYTEMNESTRA

Words, endless words, I spoke to serve my purpose.
Now I gainsay them all and feel no shame.
How can a woman work her hatred out
on him she hates and yet must seem to love,
how pile up ruin round him, fence the snare
too high to leap beyond—except by lies?
Long years ago I planned. Now it is done.
Old hatred ended. It was slow in coming,
but it came—
I stand here where I struck. So did I.
Nothing do I deny. I flung around him
a cloak, full folds, deadly folds. I caught him,
fish in a net. No way to run or fight.
Twice did I strike him and he cried out twice
and his limbs failed him and he fell, and there
I gave him the third stroke, an offering
to the god of hell who holds fast all his dead.
So there he lay and as he gasped, his blood
spouted and splashed me with black spray, a dew
of death, sweet to me as heaven's sweet rain drops
when the corn-land buds.
There stands the matter, ancient men of Argos.
Go now, and if you can, rejoice. For me,

I glory. Oh, if such a thing might be,
over the dead to pour thank-offerings,
over this dead it would be just and more.
So full of curses did he fill the cup
his house drank—but the dregs he drank himself.

LEADER

Oh, bold of tongue. We wonder at your speech.
Loud words of boasting—and the man your hus-
　　band.

CLYTEMNESTRA

Bring me to trial like any silly woman?
My heart is fearless, and you all well know
what I know. Curse me or bless me—either as you
　　will—
all one to me. Look. This is Agamemnon,
my husband, dead, struck down by my right hand,
a righteous workman. So the matter stands.

CHORUS

What evil thing, O you,
poisonous herb earth-grown, or a draught
drawn from the drifting sea,
put to your lips, has worked
　　rage for this sacrifice,
　　made you a thing accursed.
You have cast away and away shall you be cast,
　　a thing of hate to your people.

CLYTEMNESTRA

So now do you pass judgment on me? Exile—
the people's hate—cursed by men openly.
But he—you never spoke a word to cross him,

who cared no more than if a beast should die
when flocks are plenty in the fleecy fold,
and slew his daughter, dearest anguish borne
by me in travail—slew her for a charm
against the Thracian winds. Oh, never
would you drive him away from land and home,
a thing polluted. Now the deed is mine.
You are a stern judge then. I tell you plainly,
threaten what threats you will. I am content
that you shall rule if your hand prove the stronger.
But if God please the other way about,
you shall be taught, though late, the ways of wis-
　　dom.

CHORUS

Proud in your thought alway.
Scornful the words on your lips.
　Deed of blood
stamped on the maddened mind,
stain on the brow so red,
plain for all eyes to see,
branding forever shame.
Doom of dishonor, the loss of all dear,
　and blow by blow
　　paid in full for atonement.

CLYTEMNESTRA

Hear me in turn. The oath I swear is holy.
By justice for my child now consummated,
by black, blind Doom, by all the powers of hell,
to whom I offered what I killed, I swear
hope does not tread the halls of fear for me
while on my hearth a fire is still kindled

by one now true in heart to me as ever,
Aegisthus, my sure shield of confidence.
Here lies the man who scorned me—me, his wife—
the fool and tool of every shameless woman
beneath Troy's walls. Here she lies too, his slave,
got by his spear, his sibyl bed-fellow,
his paramour—God's words upon her lips,
who rubbed the galley's benches at his side.
They have their due, he thus and she the same,
her swan-song sung. His lover—there she lies.
I in my soft bed lying, shall delight,
thinking of her, still more in its smooth softness.

CHORUS

Would God that swift might come—
not after wracking pain,
not when sickness has wasted—
but swiftly come
borne by fate, unending
sleep everlasting. For he lies low now,
dearest defense to me, my master.
Much he bore
in a frail
woman's cause.
By a vile
woman's hand he fell at last.

O Helen, maddened of mind. Many men
by a woman slain,
many exceedingly.
Lives lost before Troy of her losing.
She wreathed for the last time her brow— Oh, that
garland red,

as red as blood—it will not fade—and there within
is strife that has brought to death the master.

CLYTEMNESTRA

Not death. Never pray for death—that must come—
though heavy your load.
Nor turn upon Helen your bitter wrath.
One woman—could she slay many a man?
Those lives so lost—were they lost at her hand?
That wound never closed—did she deal it?

CHORUS

Spirit of evil now
fallen upon this house,
on two kings that were kindred,
the power you wield,
hands of women wrought it,
strong as their souls—to my heart it pierces.
　　Over the body now exulting,
　　croaking your song,
　　　raven-like,
　　there you stand,
　　hateful Spirit triumphant.*

CLYTEMNESTRA

Now, judged aright—so your lips speak truth.
It is he you name,
the spirit thrice-gorged with blood of the race.
From him it has come, the thirst to lap blood.
It dwells in their flesh. Before the old wound
can be healed, there is fresh blood oozing.

* A gap here in the MS.

CHORUS

Aye—he you tell of is great,
grievous in wrath—there within abiding.
Woe— Woe. All of evil the tale,
blinding doom never glutted.
Ah me. Ah me. God's work, God's will.
All springs from him. All moves in him.
What is brought to pass apart from God for mor-
tals?
These deeds—his is the hand that wrought them.

Oh sorrow sore. O my King, O my King,
how shall I mourn you.
Or how speak from my heart that has loved you.
Caught fast in a web that a foul spider wove,
all unholy the death when your spirit fled.
So dies a slave—ah me. Like a slave you died,
by a crafty blow struck down.
Axe double-edged in a hand that spared not.

CLYTEMNESTRA

This deed my work? It is mine you proclaim?
    Look then and know me.
Here is not Agamemnon's queen. Nay, not so,
no wife of this dead man am I. In her shape
    moves the avenger,
    ancient in anger.
The grim banquet of Atreus is paid for.
    Children were slaughtered.
    And a man offered up in requital.

CHORUS

Guiltless—you—of this death?

Where is the one who will witness for you?
No— No. Yet I think another
worked with you, an avenger,
who rushes on where kin kill kin,
whose path is where dark blood flows fast,
where murdered children surely shall have venge-
      ance,
that flesh served for a father's feasting.

CLYTEMNESTRA

No! The traitorous craft of this man here dead
has brought down his house.
From his seed she sprang, that flower I bore
and wept for, Iphigenia slain.
Oh, a worthy deed and a worthy doom.
Will he boast in hell of the death he dealt,
now the score is paid
and the sword he slew with has slain him?

CHORUS

As one astray
knows not where to turn him,
so do I wander witless
where path is none.
All my house is falling.
   I fear the storm.
   Crash of thunder shakes the walls.
   The rain beats down.
   Blood—a stream, not rain drops.

Ah me— Earth, Earth, would that you held me
now—ere I had seen
   him here defeated,

slain thus in a bath silver-sided.
Who will make his grave? Who will make lament?
You? Will you dare who dared to kill him,
him who was yours?
　　Now will you weep for him?
Deeds—deeds such as these—will you blot them out
by a tear? Will the dead take your offering?
Over the grave who will speak what is due him—
God-like king? Who with tears will mourn him,
and sorrow truly—heavy-laden?

CLYTEMNESTRA

Not for you this care. Not for you is the task.
　　Mine is it only.
Hands that he fell by and died by shall bury him.
Tears? Think you that we of his household will
　　　weep?
One—one will receive him in love where he goes,
　　fitly—his daughter.
By the swift-flowing river of grief she will stand,
　　welcome to bring him.
She will hold him, enfold him, and kiss him.

CHORUS

Reproach in turn
meets reproach. I know not
who here can hold the balance.
The spoiler spoiled.
Kill—your life is forfeit.
God's law is sure.
He who wrongs, to him shall wrong
be done—in full.
From this house accursed

can any drive the seed of sin—uproot it?
No. The race fast-bound must seek its ruin.

CLYTEMNESTRA

To this, then, you come—to the law of God.
Truth is your guide now.
But for me I will swear and join in a pact
with him—with the spirit that haunts this race.
Enough. What is done, bitter hard, must be borne.
No more. Let him go—go forth from this house,
wear down, waste away, other houses,
with his death-dealing curse.
I with but little shall find full contentment,
if I drive from these halls
that frenzy when brother kills brother.

(AEGISTHUS *with attendants enters triumphantly.*)

AEGISTHUS

O kindly light. O day that leads in justice.
Now I do know that gods on high behold
the woes of earth to help and to avenge,
now that I see him lie here in the web
woven by Furies—dear sight to my eyes.
His father's crafty hand wrought, and he pays.
Atreus, his father, ruler of the land,
his throne disputed by Thyestes—
my father, his own brother—cast
him out from home and city. In his misery,
after long years had passed,
he turned back, came a suppliant to his hearth,
and won at least this mercy for himself,
a promise that he should not die and stain with blood
his fathers' halls—not he himself. Ah, but

the godless father of the dead man here,
in greeting to my father, as when one
holds merry festival after sacrifice,
made him a feast—of his own children's flesh,
the feet, the fingers, broken off. . . .*
So did he take in ignorance what then
he could not know—and fatal to the race,
as you will see, that feast has proved at last.
Poor wretch, when he had learned the deed abhor-
     rent,
he cried a great cry, falling back—spewed out
that flesh—cried out upon that house a doom
intolerable—the banquet board sent crashing
in token of his curse: "So perish all
born of this race."
And therefore is this dead man fallen here.
I planned the murder righteously,
I who, a little thing in swaddling clothes,
was cast out with my father, broken quite, at last.
But grown to manhood, justice led me back.
I was an exile, yet through me he died.
It was my hatred wove this cunning plot.
Now let death come. Why care when my own eyes
have seen him caught fast in the net of justice.

LEADER

Aegisthus, insult to grief I do detest.
Your plan, yours only, so you boast, this murder.
This piteous death your work. Justice still lives.

* A gap in the MS. is indicated here.

Your time will come, be sure, when there shall
  gather
from out the town all men to curse—throw stones—

AEGISTHUS

What! A poor oarsman at his lowly post
deep in the ship, dares speak threats to the master?
Such words from you to me? Ah—you are old.
Gray hairs find learning bitter yet they must be
  taught
to be discreet, and bonds and hunger pain
are admirable teachers—physicians truly
to help the old to wisdom. You have eyes
and do not see things? Why kick
against the pricks? Your hurt alone—no more.

LEADER

(*turning from him to* CLYTEMNESTRA.)
O woman, waiting, watching in the house
for an army coming home from war. Their captain
  came.
His bed you shamed—his death contrived, O woman.

AEGISTHUS

These too are words that shall be paid with tears.
The opposite to Orpheus' tongue is yours.
He led all things by his enchanting song.
Your silly talk, that can but irritate,
shall lead you where you would not be.
You will be milder soon.

LEADER

You, master here in Argos—you, who planned
a death and never dared to do it?

AEGISTHUS

To trick him was his wife's part. That was clear.
All knew I was his enemy of old.
His goods are mine now. With gold a man can rule.
I shall make trial of the people. Yoke
and heavily him who will not obey.
I'll have no trace-horse full of barley, running riot.
Hunger and hateful darkness, two who dwell
together, soon will see him tamed.

LEADER

Shame on your coward's soul who did not kill
the man yourself but left him to a woman.
Oh, vile pollution of this land, polluting
the very gods. But yet Orestes lives.
Oh, may kind fortune lead him home again
to victory, to vengeance, on these two.

AEGISTHUS

Thus to speak, then, you are minded, thus to do? *
    You shall be taught.
Ho there, men-at-arms, old comrades. Work for you
    and to your hand.
    (*Spearsmen rush in and threaten the* CHORUS.)

LEADER

Up, men all. Each one stand ready. Draw, now.
    Sword in hand. Stand firm.

* The meter here changes from the customary six-foot line
to one of eight feet.

AEGISTHUS

Hand on hilt, I too am ready. Death be judge. I am
content.

LEADER

Death! Your word. We take the omen. Gladly welcome it for you.

(*A fight is imminent. Before they can come to
blows* CLYTEMNESTRA *hurries down the steps and
stands between the two bands. She turns to* AEGIS-
THUS.)

CLYTEMNESTRA

Peace, oh peace, my best-beloved. No more evil
now. Enough.

What is done will bring hard reaping, heavy har-
vesting, not good.

Trouble in full measure here is. No more blood for
you and me.

Go your ways, old men, in honor. To your homes
now, everyone.

Destiny determined all here. Yield before you suffer
harm.

What we did was what was fated. Oh, if this could
be the end.

Sorely smitten though I am, brought low beneath
God's heavy hand,

these things I can bear. No more. A woman's word,
if men will hear.

AEGISTHUS

Let them go in peace, and safely sow a crop of evil
speech?

Casting sneering words against me, tempting for-
tune? Dangerous.
I forgive this insult—outrage? I their king now?
They shall learn—

LEADER

Evil men are never those the Argive breed will
cringe before—

AEGISTHUS

Wait. The days are near when I will send for you
and you will come.
(*He turns away, lowering his spear.*)

LEADER

Never—if fate guides Orestes to come home at last—
at last.

AEGISTHUS

Well I know myself the exile's food to feed the
spirit—hope.

LEADER

Keep your course. Wax fat. Dishonor justice. You
have power—now.

AEGISTHUS

Know that folly always suffers. You will pay full
price to me.

LEADER

Cocks crow loudest to their hens—and braggarts do
the like, men say.

CLYTEMNESTRA

Dogs will bark. Who cares to listen? What avails
   this foolish speech?
You and I are lords here. We two now will order
   all things well.

Books That Live

The Norton imprint on a
book means that in the
publisher's estimation it
is a book not for a single
season but for the years.

W · W · NORTON & CO · INC.

NEW YORK